baia
the castle, museum and archaeological sites

quick guide

text by
Paola Miniero

baia
the castle, museum and archaeological sites

electa napoli soprintendenza
per i beni archeologici
di napoli e caserta

Museo Archeologico
dei Campi Flegrei

Scientific Directors
Stefano De Caro
Paola Miniero

Graphic Archive
Eva Nardella
Eduardo Scognamiglio

Photographic Archive
Alessandra Villone

Editoriale Services
Marco de Gemmis
Floriana Miele

Commercial Services
Stefania Saviano

Electa Napoli

Managing Editor
Silvia Cassani

Graphic design and layout
Enrica D'Aguanno
Nadia Bronzuto

Photographs
Archivio fotografico
della Soprintendenza
per i Beni Archeologici
di Napoli e Caserta;
Riccardo Giordano;
Enrico Guglielmo (p. 14);
Nicola Severino (pp. 23, 73)
Underwater photographs:
Eduardo Scognamiglio (p. 22)

On the cover:
Statue of Antonia Minor, detail
A. Joli, *Baia*, detail.
Private collection

Contents

Baia in history

Roman Baiae was renowned as a seaside resort and spa town from the 2nd century BC to the 3rd century AD. The site today would be unrecognisable to Romans, partly because the coastline has subsided and been greatly altered by the volcanic phenomenon of bradyseism, and also because much of the ancient architecture has succumbed to property developers, particularly in recent decades. Nonetheless the extant remains of bathing establishments and residential complexes can give us a very good idea of why this resort was once so prestigious.

As Pliny the Elder observed during the first century AD (*Naturalis Historia* II, 17), few places on earth have been blessed with such a profusion of natural resources. Baia has always had a great number of mineral springs, offering a range of therapeutic properties. Then it lies in a beautiful natural setting and has a particularly temperate climate. These features were frequently extolled by ancient authors, and they were the key to its development as a fashionable resort for the Roman aristocracy and emperors during the last two centuries of the Republic and the first three centuries of the Empire.

We find the first mention of Baia in a work by Lycophron dating from the 3rd century BC. In his account of the voyage of Ulysses, he identifies it as the place of burial of the steersman Baios. In archaic times it was a landing place giving access to the important Greek colony at Cumae. It was never a *municipium* with an autonomous status, and remained under the jurisdiction of Cumae. The Greek author Strabo, in his work *Geographica* V, 4, 5, spoke of the tribe of the Cimmerii on Lake Avernus, not far from Baia. They lived in underground caverns and supported themselves on the income generated by the oracle of the dead (associated with Lake Avernus) and by quarrying the tuff rock. This account is corroborated by the numerous passageways bored through the outcrops of tuff that occur round the lakes of Avernus and Lucrinus and along the coast as far as Baia. Some of these tunnels undoubtedly date back to ancient times, and were created either to extract building material (notably the volcanic ash pozzolana) or to exploit the hot vapours.

Roman times. Development of spa activity and residential facilities
As early as 176 BC Baia had

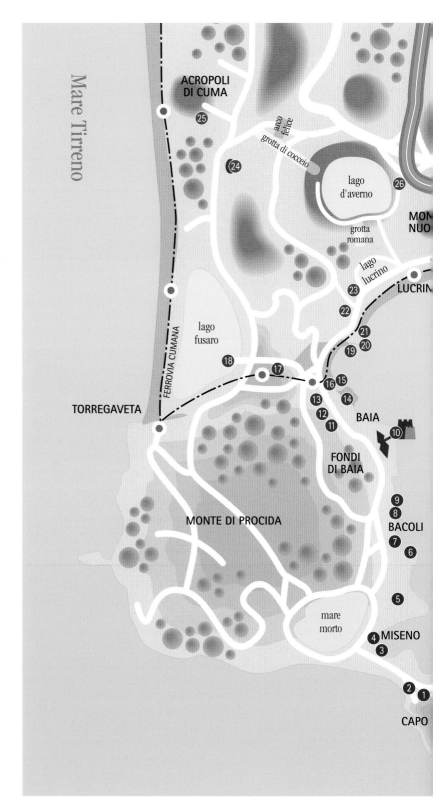

The archaeological sites in Baia, Bacoli and Miseno

Mare Tirreno

ACROPOLI
DI CUMA

arco felice

grotta di cocceio

lago
d'averno

grotta
romana

MON
NUO

lago
lucrino

LUCRIN

FERROVIA CUMANA

lago
fusaro

TORREGAVETA

BAIA

FONDI
DI BAIA

BACOLI

MONTE DI PROCIDA

mare
morto

MISENO

CAPO

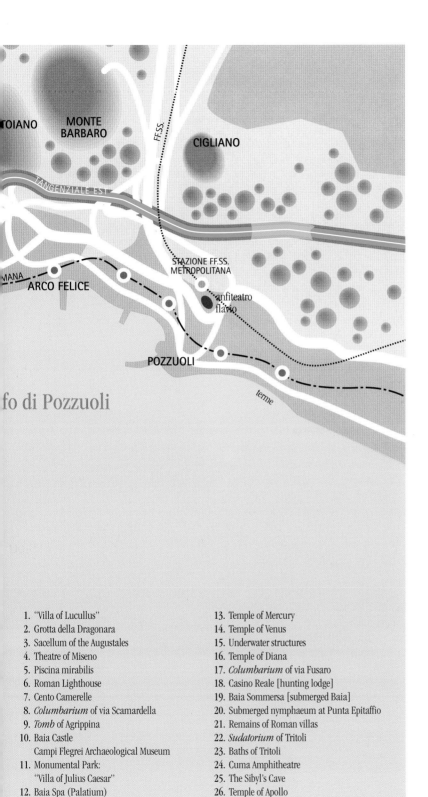

OIANO

MONTE BARBARO

CIGLIANO

FF.SS.

TANGENZIALE EST

MANA

ARCO FELICE

STAZIONE FF.SS.
METROPOLITANA

anfiteatro flavio

POZZUOLI

fo di Pozzuoli

terme

<table>
<tr><td>1. "Villa of Lucullus"</td><td>13. Temple of Mercury</td></tr>
<tr><td>2. Grotta della Dragonara</td><td>14. Temple of Venus</td></tr>
<tr><td>3. Sacellum of the Augustales</td><td>15. Underwater structures</td></tr>
<tr><td>4. Theatre of Miseno</td><td>16. Temple of Diana</td></tr>
<tr><td>5. Piscina mirabilis</td><td>17. Columbarium of via Fusaro</td></tr>
<tr><td>6. Roman Lighthouse</td><td>18. Casino Reale [hunting lodge]</td></tr>
<tr><td>7. Cento Camerelle</td><td>19. Baia Sommersa [submerged Baia]</td></tr>
<tr><td>8. Columbarium of via Scamardella</td><td>20. Submerged nymphaeum at Punta Epitaffio</td></tr>
<tr><td>9. Tomb of Agrippina</td><td>21. Remains of Roman villas</td></tr>
<tr><td>10. Baia Castle
Campi Flegrei Archaeological Museum</td><td>22. Sudatorium of Tritoli</td></tr>
<tr><td>11. Monumental Park:
"Villa of Julius Caesar"</td><td>23. Baths of Tritoli
24. Cuma Amphitheatre</td></tr>
<tr><td>12. Baia Spa (Palatium)</td><td>25. The Sibyl's Cave
26. Temple of Apollo</td></tr>
</table>

acquired a reputation as a spa. The historian Titus Livius (XLI, 16) records that the consul Caius Cornelius Scipio Hispallo came for a cure in the *aquae Cumanae*, Baia being part of the territory of Cumae. The therapeutic properties of the waters were complemented by steam baths, taken in a specially built chamber known as the *laconicum*. The hot dry air currents were held to drive out the humours that caused illnesses, after which the bather would wash in the mineral springs. The oldest examples of such chambers known to us are at Baia. The *Sudatorium* of Tritoli, for example, was hollowed out of the cliff and heated by a current coming up a duct through the tuff some 60 metres long.

Writing early in the first century AD, Celsus mentioned the specially built *sudatoria* "in the myrtle groves above Baia" in a medical treatise (II, 7). We can identify these as the more sophisticated constructions built against the cliff face rising up behind Baia. The so-called Minor Baths have a *laconicum* in the form of a rotunda, dating from the mid-1st century BC and featuring the hypocaust system with *suspensurae*: the chamber was heated by feeding hot air under the floor and up flues inside the walls. This feature revolutionised the construction of Roman baths. Pliny the Elder referred to the new system as *pensilia balinea* (*Naturalis Historia* IX, 168). Its invention, *in Baiano* at the beginning of the first century BC, is attributed to Caius Sergius Orata, a prosperous entrepreneur best known for his fish farms on Lake Lucrinus and his novel method of

breeding oysters. The historian Valerius Maximus (IX, I.1) records that the oysters were raised in artificial basins on rows of terracotta pantiles coated with lime and sand, just as happens today in the oysterbeds of northern France. This development of the spa activity and oyster farming gave rise to a great demand for housing, and in the space of a few decades during the 1st century BC the coastline and hillside around Baia were covered with villas. Writing in the Augustan era, Strabo spoke of "a city that has grown up with the addition of royal residences and other buildings, quite as large as Puteoli", while Horace condemned what he called "this *voluptas*

aedificandi", with people building villas not only on all the available land but also out over the sea. He may well have been referring to the villa of Lucius Calpurnius Piso (the only one we can identify with certainty thanks to lead water pipes stamped with his name). The whole eastern sector of this villa with its colonnades and fish tanks was built out over the sea on a concrete platform.

Literary sources provide us with the names of some fifty well-to-do individuals who owned villas in the Bay of Naples during the first century BC, particularly in and around Baia. These include Marcus Antonius, Licinius Crassus, Quintus Caecilius Metellus Celere, his wife Clodia, Publius Cornelius Dolabella, Quintus Hortensius Hortalus, Caius Marius, Julius Caesar, Lucullus, Pompeius Magnus and Lucius Calpurnius Piso. Most of these dwellings would have been *villae maritimae*, built to enable their owners to indulge in *otium* and *balnea* (leisure and bathing activities), but also providing an income from the tanks used for fish and oyster farming. The shellfish coming from Lake Lucrinus were celebrated right up until the demise of the Roman Empire. Not much remains of these buildings, and only that of L. C. Piso can be definitely attributed to one of the above owners. This villa, like the others originally built on the seashore, now lies under the sea, while those built on the hillside tended to be confiscated and become Imperial property. They were then either knocked down or incorporated into one of the emperor's own residences, making them unrecognisable today. One other villa which we may be able to identify on the basis of a passage in Tacitus (*Annales*, XIV, 9) is that of Julius Caesar, currently being excavated in the upper section of the Monumental Park of Baia.

There are no end of references in literary sources to the bathing establishments of Baia, which were at the height of fashion for several centuries. Precious little now remains of them, as a result above all of quarrying for the raw material for pozzolana cement over the last fifty years. All we can still see of the whole complex are the so-called Baths (Terme). Some scholars, including Maiuri and de Franciscis, believe that this building was actually the *Palatium* or

View of the coastline of Baia depicted on 3rd-4th century glass flasks found in Warsaw, Populonia and Ampurias. The main landmarks are shown. The term palatium *could indicate the Imperial palace, corresponding to the ruins traditionally known as the "Terme di Baia"*

Imperial residence. Baia was the resort of emperors during the 1st - 3rd centuries AD, and witnessed some memorable exploits. Cassius Dio (59, 17, 2 & 11) tells us that in 39 AD Caligula (37-41 AD) had a bridge of boats built across the bay of Puteoli, to outdo the one assembled across the Hellespont by Darius, king of the Persians. He rode across it on horseback, preceded on foot by a subjugated Parthian prince also named Darius. The presence of Claudius (41-54 AD) in Baia is recorded in the edict he issued from the *praetorium* here granting the rights of citizenship to the Anauni, a pre-Roman people whose name is conserved in the toponym Val di Non, in the foothills of the Alps. Nero (54-68 AD) was particularly attached to the region of the Phlegraean Fields and Baia. His ambition was to link it to Rome by means of a gigantic canal ("*fossam ab Averno Ostiamque usquam*": Suetonius, *Nero*, 31, 3) measuring

160 Roman miles in length and wide enough to allow two quinqueremes to pass. It was supposed to start at Portus Iulius, situated between Lakes Lucrinus and Avernus, and finish at the port of Ostiae at the mouth of the Tiber, giving access to Rome without the uncertainties of sailing up the coast. The project was never realised, but traces of parts of the canal were discovered by Werner Johannowsky, and Fausto Zevi has identified the entrance to it with a canal leading out of Portus Iulius, now underwater. We learn from Tacitus and Suetonius that Nero assembled an enormous property at Baia, stopping at nothing to take possession of the finest villas, including those of his mother Agrippina, of his aunt Domitia Lepida, whom he had assassinated, and of the Piso family, which he confiscated after discovering that they had plotted to kill him. However, the imperial history of Baia was not all infamous: it also

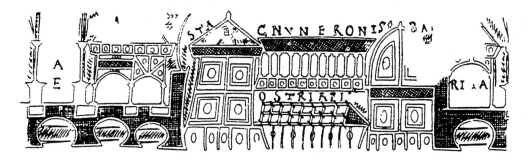

saw examples of filial devotion. The emperor Hadrian died here in 138 AD, and his adopted son Antoninus Pius (138-161 AD) established the annual games of the *Eusebeia* in his honour. In the following century Alexander Severus (222-235 AD) commemorated his mother Mamea by having a palace built round an ornamental lake, "*palatium cum stagno*", and other water features, *stagna stupenda,* for other members of his family. The two terms *palatium* and *stagnum* are found on three glass flasks manufactured in Puteoli in the 3rd or 4th century AD. Such flasks seem to have been souvenirs bought by people visiting the Phlegraean Fields, and specimens have come to light in various parts of the Roman Empire. The three in question were found in Warsaw, Populonia and Ampurias and bear schematic views of the coastline between Baia and Misenum with the main landmarks. Although the landmarks are identified by captions, they cannot be readily identified with existing features in the bay: *stagnum Neronis* (a fish-pool or port flanked by moles); *ostriaria* (ponds for breeding mussels); a *palatium*, figuring only on the flask found at Populonia, clearly an allusion to the Palatine hill in Rome, where the residence

of the Flavian imperial family was located; a second *stagnum* with no name attached; and also *silvae* (woods).

Recent underwater research carried out off the Aragonese Castle by G. Di Fraia, E. Scognamiglio and N. Lombardo has identified a complex of fish ponds with features which correspond to the *stagnum Neronis* and *ostriaria* as depicted on the flasks: the semicircular layout of the former, and poles implanted in the seabed to which the mussels clung and a series of canals ensuring the through-put of seawater for the latter. If these are in fact the remains of these two landmarks, the anonymous *stagnum* on the Warsaw flask could refer to the pools created by Alexander Severus; remains of buildings dating from this emperor's reign came to light when the harbour was dredged during the 1920s. All the space between these two fish pools is occupied on the flask found at Populonia by the word *palatium*, with *ostriaria* beneath it, suggesting an imperial residence in a commanding position overlooking the other landmarks. This could well be the complex of ruins known as the Terme di Baia, which must have been one of the most striking features on the coastline during the 4th century AD.

*Aerial view
of the castle of Baia*

The site probably extended as far as Punta del Castello, and would have been densely wooded, hence the caption *"silvae"* on the vase found in Warsaw. Furthermore Fausto Zevi has suggested that there is a strong link between the *palatium* in Baia and the *Domus Aurea* in Rome, the highly extravagant complex of buildings put up by Nero after fire had destroyed the oldest aristocratic residences on the Palatine hill. The only remains to have come down to us of the *Domus Aurea* are incorporated into the Baths of Trajan, but recent excavations indicate that it comprised a number of separate buildings dotted over the hillside at differing heights, round a hollow known as the *stagnum maris* or "sea pool", where subsequently Vespasian was to erect the Colosseum. There can be no denying the similarity with the imperial palace in Baia, which may well have been taken as the model for Nero's extravaganza in Rome (Zevi 1996). This would not be the only case of an architectonic structure being developed first in Baia and subsequently exploited in Rome. The so-called Tempio di Mercurio is the oldest of the three impressive domed buildings that have come down to us in Baia; it was constructed at least a century before the Pantheon was built by Hadrian. Again, imperial commissions of sculpture could be met just as well in Baia as in Rome, as we know from the sculptures adorning the *nymphaeum* of Punta Epitaffio, done in a local workshop for the emperor Claudius. There are in fact records of a workshop of sculptors turning out copies which may have been located in the imperial residence itself; it was active from the Augustan era until late in the reign of Antoninus (up to about 160 AD).

The scant remains of this whole complex do not allow us to identify the various buildings which once stood along the seafront or link them to this or that emperor, or even be sure what was public property and what private. This is due in part to the effects of bradyseism, which has caused the sea level to rise, and also to the wholesale destruction carried out in the recent past in building the coast road and the harbour quay. There are nonetheless two elements which point to the presence of imperial residences: the highly elaborate *nymphaeum-triclinium* created for the emperor Claudius off Punta Epitaffio, and the thirteen *fistulae aquarie* (water pipes) recovered from the sea during the construction of the quay in the 1920s, stamped with the names of the emperors Domitian, Septimius Severus, Alexander Severus and above all Caracalla.

Late ancient times and the Middle Ages

Archaeological evidence relating to the period when the *nymphaeum* of Punta Epitaffio was abandoned indicates that by the 4th century AD bradyseism was already causing the shoreline to sink. Yet there is nothing to suggest that Baia went into decline for at least another century. One Simmacus is known to have possessed various villas in the Phlegraean Fields, one near Lake Lucrinus. There were undoubtedly villas on the hillside of Tritoli overlooking the lake: early in the 20th century a floor mosaic featuring a hunting scene was found here, dating from the 4th century. It was acquired by a private collector, and is now in the J. P. Getty Museum.

Following the fall of the Roman Empire in 476 AD, this region too was open to raiding by successive waves of Visigoths, Vandals and

Goths. They did not destroy the bathing establishments, for we know that some barbarian chiefs came to Baia to take the waters. Writing in the 6th century, Cassiodorus spoke of Baia as a pleasant resort. In an apocryphal version of the *Acts of the Apostles* (XXVIII, 12) we learn of the divine punishment called down by St Paul on the inhabitants of Puteoli for sentencing him to death: the city sank into the sea, "to the depth of an ell … at a place called Baia". This must be a reference to an episode of bradyseism, but at this time the phenomenon was relatively minor, since the ancient

Miniature showing the "Baths of the Sun and the Moon" from the codex De Balneis Puteolanis by Pietro da Eboli. Rome, Biblioteca Angelica

buildings were still perfectly visible, like "a monument in the sea". Stratigraphic data show that the period of maximum increase of the sea level came in the tenth century, when the territory became covered with swamps and scrub vegetation, although this did not avert invasions by the Longobards and the Saracens.

In the Middle Ages Baia was still famed for its waters, as we learn from works by Giovanni Diacono (10th century), Beniamino da Tudela and Corrado di Querfurt (12th century). The Swabian king Friedrich II took the waters here in 1227 on his return from Brindisi, and ordered some of the facilities to be renovated. A clerk at the Swabian court, Pietro da Eboli, wrote a guide to the various mineral waters in the form of a short poem entitled *De Balneis Puteolanis*, of which several manuscript copies have survived, decorated with precious miniatures. The therapeutic properties of springs at both Puteoli and Baia are described, in what was apparently an attempt to undermine the prestige of the medical school in Salerno. The *Cronaca di Partenope* narrates that the worthy doctors of Salerno were so incensed that they carried out a punitive raid, damaging some of the facilities in Baia, but incurred divine retribution and perished at sea on their way home.

The strategic importance of the port of Baia was apparent to the Aragonese rulers of Naples (1442-1501). They built a system of coastal defences which included a fortress (1490-1493), and this was enlarged to constitute the castle we know today by the Spanish Viceroy Pedro di Toledo. It was during his rule in Naples, on 29th September 1538, that a dramatic volcanic eruption produced Monte Nuovo: the emergence of this "new hill" transformed the coastline between Baia and Pozzuoli, obliterating the coast road and the village of Tripergole. A subsequent viceroy, Pietro di Aragona (1666-1671), set about restoring the fortunes of Baia with various public works schemes including the rebuilding of the coast road (Via Aragonia) and the renovation of the spa facilities. They were placed under the supervision of Sebastiano Bartolo, a doctor from Irpinia, and gradually attracted a regular clientele.

At the same time the interest taken by scholars and dilettantes in antiquity, prompted by the spread of humanism, resulted in publications of drawings and guides featuring the monuments of the Phlegraean Fields region. The striking ruins of ancient Baia made it one of the mandatory sights for travellers drawn from all over Europe, and the port and castle maintained a certain military importance up until the Unification of Italy.

From Lucrino to Baia

The hill of Tritoli and its archaeological remains

The hill of Tritoli, rising to about 40 metres above the current sea level, marks the northern edge of the territory of Baia. Beyond it stretches Lake Lucrinus, now considerably smaller than it was in ancient times. Strabo records (V 4, 6) that the lake was separated from the sea by a strip of land one mile in length and wide enough to allow carts to pass. This was the Via Herculea (or Herculanea or Heraclea), a road alleged to have been built by Hercules himself: the Greek historians Ephoros and Timaeus state that this road dates back at least to the second half of the 4th century BC. The Roman Senate had the isthmus strengthened with an embankment during the first century BC to protect the fish and oyster farms on Lake Lucrinus. It can be identified in aerial photographs, running to the south-west and crossing the canal leading into Portus Iulius. It probably continued along the line of the Secca Fumosa, between 450 and 525 metres offshore with respect to the present shoreline, in the direction of Punta Epitaffio, where a stretch of paved road has been found in

the sea at a depth of 3.75 metres. This sector of coast has undergone the greatest transformations since Roman times, rising and sinking with the successive phases of bradyseism. A recent geo-archaeological survey carried out beneath Via Montegrillo during construction work on the Cumana railway showed that there was once a lagoon here, with water bathing the lower slopes of the hillside. The current toponym "Stufe di Nerone" appears in Suetonius and recalls the swimming pool created for Nero between Misenum and Lake Avernus (Suetonius, *Nero* XXI), fed by all the hot springs in the neighbourhood. These springs, which are still active, caught the imagination of travellers and featured frequently in engravings. Exploited by the Romans, they were rediscovered in medieval times. The poem *De Balneis Puteolanis* names several of them: *Balneum Silvianae, Trituli, San Georgii, Pugillus, Petrolei,* each a small bathing establishment. The latter three stood on the shore and are now underwater. If you go by boat from Lucrino to Punta Epitaffio you can feel that in some places the sea is quite hot on

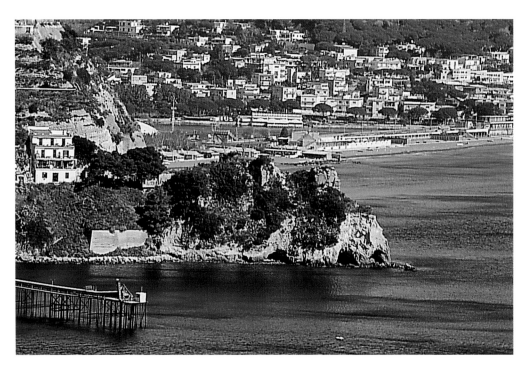

Aerial view of Punta Epitaffio, where the Nymphaeum of the emperor Claudius was uncovered during underwater excavations. Now on display in the Archaeological Museum of the Phlegraean Fields

Facing page: Model of the Nymphaeum of Punta Epitaffio in the Archaeological Museum of the Phlegraean Fields in the castle of Baia

account of springs welling up from the seabed. The archaeological remains we describe below are all that is left of these bathing establishments, and are not generally accessible because they are located on private property. One part of an *exedra-nymphaeum* in *opus caementicium* with traces of the original plasterwork dating from the 2nd century AD has been incorporated into the modern bathing establishment "Stufe di Nerone Club". This stands on the site of the medieval baths known as the Bagno del Figulaio, built over the spring called *Balneum Silvianae,* which still produces a constant jet of heat at between 45° and 50°C.

Sudatorium of Tritoli ("Stufe di Nerone")

The original steam bath (*sudatorium*) of Tritoli dates back to the late Republican era. It stood on the road to Baia, Via Aragonia, built in a covered gallery hewn out of the south-west flank of the hillside and traditionally known as the Grotta di Baia or Spanish Gallery, having been created by the Viceroy Don Pedro Antonio d'Aragona (1666-1671) to link Puteoli and Baia. A short stretch of the road is still visible, used as a shelter for cattle. The remains of this steam bath can still be recognised today, although it has been incorporated into a private house and whitewashed. The "stews of Nero" consisted in chambers hollowed out of the tuff, provided in medieval times with stone benches. A tunnel stretches down into the cliff which can be followed with great caution for some 70 metres, leading to the hot spring below sea level, still active at a temperature of about 60°C.

Balneum Tritoli (Baths of Tritoli)

Behind the small church of San Filippo, beneath what is now Via

Temporini, there is a large rectangular chamber (measuring 8.70 x 17m) hollowed out of the tuff, now entirely below ground apart from the barrel vaulted roof. We know from an engraving made by Paoli in about 1768 that the vault was decorated with large octagonal coffers. The original structure of this chamber, built over a hot spring, goes back to Roman times. In ancient times the whole of this hillside, from the new tunnel of the Cumana railway to the easternmost slope above Punta Epitaffio, was terraced with large barrel vaulted chambers in *opus reticulatum* built against the hillside in several tiers. Recently a landslip has exposed three levels of these substructions (at between 10 and 36 metres above sea level). Some led into other rooms and corridors excavated in the hill. This is all that remains of the villas built on this hillside during the Augustan era. The mosaic featuring a hunting scene, dating from a slightly later period, would have belonged to one such villa. It was found in 1901 in the locality Scalandrone and is now in the J.P. Getty Museum in California.

Punta Epitaffio and the underwater nymphaeum

The "Point of the Epitaph" is so-called on account of an inscription found here (the third in a series) in which the physician Sebastiano Bartolo enumerated the various baths of Baia. The plaque was set up in 1668 at the instigation of the Viceroy Don Pedro Antonio d'Aragona: one of the other two can be seen in the wall at Porta Napoli in Pozzuoli. This point is today the northernmost tip of the bay of Baia. In ancient times the coastline was some 400 metres further forward, and the coastal strip in front of the hillside would have been full of buildings now lying under water. The most significant structure known to us is

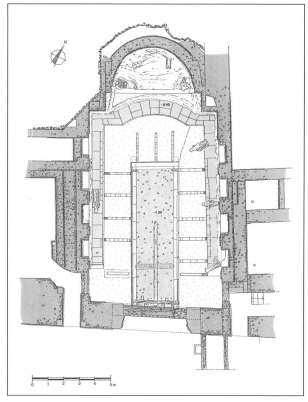

Ground-plan of the Nymphaeum of Punta Epitaffio

the nymphaeum of the emperor Claudius, the first ancient ruin to be excavated by an archaeologist (Piero A. Gianfrotta) working as a scuba diver, under the supervision of Fausto Zevi and Bernard Andreae. All the finds from the nymphaeum are on display in the Archaeological Museum of the Phlegraean Fields (see p. 57). The hillside of Punta Epitaffio is now liable to landslips on account of erosion by the wind and sea; archaeological remains that once stood along the ridge and extended down the hillside have fallen into the sea.

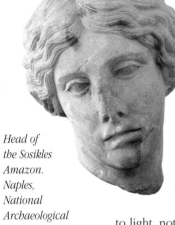

Head of the Sosikles Amazon. Naples, National Archaeological Museum

Baianus lacus and the underwater structures in the port of Baia

During dredging in the port of Baia in the 1920s various ancient objects came to light, notably two statues in Pentelic marble, one of Aphrodite (the type known as the *"Hera Borghese"*, signed by the Athenian sculptor Aphrodisios), the other an Amazon head of the *Sosikles* type, created in a local workshop, both now in the National Archaeological Museum of Naples. In the 1950s underwater research was carried out by N. Lamboglia and A. Mauri, but apart from the retrieval in 1969 of the statues of Ulysses and a companion, not much was achieved. Then in the early 1980s the nymphaeum of Punta Epitaffio was thoroughly investigated, and since then the divers Gennaro Di Fraia, Eduardo Scognamiglio and Nicolai

Lombardo have verified the advanced location of the shoreline in ancient times, with a highly developed coastal strip surrounding an inner basin called the *Baianus lacus,* which was much smaller than the bay as it is today.

This inner basin was reached by a wide canal (f), now partially silted up but still visible. In Roman times the sea proper was 370 metres off the present shoreline, as indicated by a row of 25 *pilae* (d), massive blocks of *opus caementicium* and tuff fragments each measuring about 7 x 8 metres. From the sides they have the appearance of *opus reticulatum*; they formed an artificial breakwater protecting the seaward quarters of a large residential building located some 130 metres from Punta Epitaffio (c). At the beginning of the first century AD this villa belonged to the Pisoni, as we know from the lead piping found here, stamped with the name of the first owner, *L Calpurni.* Lucius Calpurnius Piso was the leader of a plot to assassinate Nero hatched here in Baia, and when the plot was exposed the villa was probably confiscated, added to the imperial estate and completely restructured during the 2nd century AD. It was laid out around a grand central courtyard, rectangular in shape, with a monumental façade facing Punta Epitaffio, featuring curvilinear alcoves framed by semicolumns and clad in marble, stucco and plaster work. The portico round the inner courtyard was also sumptuously decorated: the north and east sides had alternate semicircular and rectangular apses in *opus reticulatum* in the Augustan style;

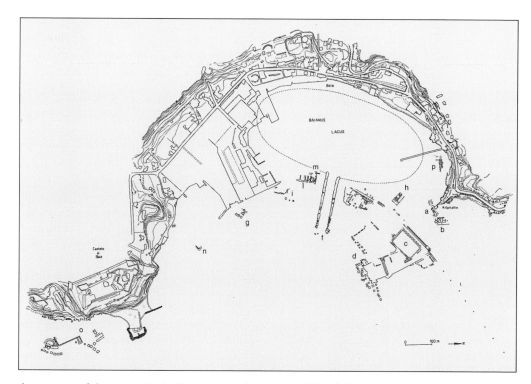

the interior of the west side had rectangular alcoves framed by semicolumns in *opus latericium*; and the south, subjected over the centuries to the assault of the sea, a marble colonnade. The south-facing quarters of the villa were built out over the sea on a concrete platform, with two landing-stages, pools for breeding fish and shellfish and water tanks. Between this villa and the nymphaeum (a) there was another building originating from the Flavian era (b) and restructured in the 3rd century AD. It comprised a baths suite with the conventional sequence of *calidarium*, *tepidarium* and *frigidarium*, and opposite this a nymphaeum on a plinth resembling an exedra, unique of its kind. This gave onto the paved road which led to the nymphaeum of the emperor Claudius (a).

Another nucleus of ruins (e-h) stands on a road that led up to the Villa of L.C. Piso, now covered in sand. To one side is a bathing establishment and facing it a row of *tabernae* (shops) and a villa, of which at present only the entrance has been identified. This consists in a porch or prothyrum leading into the atrium and a cubiculum with mosaic flooring. Immediately behind these structures, in what was perhaps a garden, a statue was recently found, now on display in the Castle of Baia. It represents a woman seated on a throne, but is lacking the head and has been completely corroded by stone-boring mussels.

The letter (g) indicates remains lying off the present shipyards, comprising a concrete platform and three *pilae*. A section of the foundations of the original quay has recently been identified in the sea between the southern side of

Archaeological map of the underwater remains of Baia

Above: *Underwater villa with porch (e): mosaic flooring in the cubiculum*

Underwater villa of Lucius Calpurnius Piso (c): brick semicolumn from the portico

Below: *Remains of wooden shuttering from the foundations of a pier (m)*

the access canal and the current jetty of the Omlin shipyard. Between the quay and the inner basin the remains of two buildings have been found (l-m), but they have been so badly damaged by traffic using the port that there are few clues as to their identity. One (m) conserves fragments of the wooden shuttering used in building the foundations, the first evidence we have of a construction method using vertical stanchions fixed to the flooring by means of pairs of nails.

In the sea off the Castle of Baia itself a vast area (o) is being investigated comprising fish pools, porticoes and pavilions, including a semicircular building, protected by enormous *pilae* with a core of *opus caementicium* faced with a sort of *opus reticulatum*, indicating that there must have been a quay here too. This could be the site of the *stagna Neronis* which feature on the flasks from Warsaw and Ampurias described above. Other archaeological remains (p) have been identified from aerial photographs and have yet to be investigated, while still others (n) lie beneath the carcasses of old

ships left to rot in a veritable "maritime knacker's yard", now gradually being cleaned up. What we have described is in fact only the visible portion – standing free of the sand – of an archaeological treasure trove which covers a larger area than the remains on land. This could become a substantial underwater archaeological park, for the structures lie at no great depth and are very striking when seen from a craft with a transparent bottom, as has already been proved on various occasions. For this asset to be conserved and exploited, a stop must be put to commercial traffic in the port and resources invested in a form of tourism that is compatible with the archaeological heritage.

The only ancient building that stands up out of the sea is known as Villa Gallo, after the modern house built on top of it. It was constructed on at least three storeys, of which only the middle one gives an idea of the original structure. Above only the floor level survives, while the bottom storey is under water up to the vaults. It is not clear whether this was a villa or a bathing establishment, although the fact that in medieval times this was the site of the "Bagno del Sole e della Luna" favours the latter hypothesis. There is a striking similarity with the villa known as the "Palazzo degli Spiriti" on the promontory of Posillipo.

The "Temples" or "Trugli"
Tempio di Mercurio: access from the Archaeological Park (see below for opening times).
Tempio di Venere: visit by arrangement with the Ufficio

*Archeologico di Baia
(tel/fax 081.5233797).
Tempio di Diana: closed during
restoration work.*
The residential and recreational
building boom in Baia at the start
of the Imperial era gave rise to
innovations in architecture which
Pliny referred to as *mos baianum*
(in the style of Baia). The most
characteristic feature of this
experimentation was the
construction of large vaulted
rotundas. Their sheer size
convinced the adepts of the Grand
Tour that they must be "temples",
duly ascribed to the divinities
Mercury, Venus and Diana, while
the locals referred to them as
"trugli" or troglodytic dwellings. In
fact they were large steam baths.
Their construction was made
possible by the great invention of
Roman builders, *opus
caementicium,* which ensured a
solid load-bearing structure. It was
made up of tuff stones
incorporated into a special mortar
mixed with pozzolana (*pulvis
puteolanus*). This volcanic ash,
lightweight and readily available in
the Phlegraean Fields region, made
a hydraulic cement which was
uniquely suited to constructing not
only curved domes but also dykes,
bridges and jetties, since it could
solidify under water.
The first example of these large-
scale structures was the "**Tempio di
Mercurio**", whose form owed
something to the *laconica* (round
steam baths) known to us from
Pompeii and Herculaneum.
Standing in the Archaeological
Park, it was built around the
beginning of the Christian era at
the bottom of the hillside, near a
mineral spring which was hot and
sulphurous. In medieval times the
baths on this site were known as

*View of a Roman
villa partly
underwater known
as "Villa Gallo"*

The Tempio di Mercurio in an engraving by P.E. Paoli (circa 1768)

Tempio di Mercurio, exterior. The external pile reinforcing the load-bearing wall is clearly visible

Tempio di Mercurio, internal chamber now under water due to bradyseism

Facing page:
The Tempio di Venere, ground-plan. The building dates from the reign of the emperor Hadrian (117-138 AD)

Tempio di Venere. In the background, the Archaeological Park

the "Baths of the Bishop's Spring", perhaps recalling the visit of the prelate Corrado de Querfurt in 1194. As a result of bradyseism only the dome of the building is now above ground, and our knowledge of it is based on a famous engraving by Paoli (circa 1768). This shows the chamber already partly under water, with a visitor being carried across on the shoulders of a local. There are four large segmental arches located on perpendicular axes; the one against the hillside leads through to an apse. According to the 19th century scholars Panvini and Paolini, this is where the mineral water flowed into the chamber, issuing from inside the hillside. The chamber was one large *natatio* (pool) where people could immerse themselves in the therapeutic waters. The four arches were adorned with ornamental recesses and the four rows of holes in the walls held in place marble facing. Friedrich Rakob (1988) identifies the Tempio di Mercurio as the first stage in the Romans' development of the dome. The pool, measuring 25.66 metres in diameter, was originally uncovered, and the chamber comprised a round wall in *opus caementicium* faced in *opus reticulatum*. Before the large semicircular dome could be added, this had to be flanked by a second wall of the same structure and dimensions, reinforced with a row of external pillars on the eastern side. The latter detail indicates that this form of architecture was still at

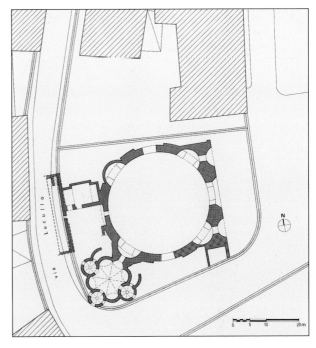

Tempio di Venere seen from the Monumental Park

a rudimental stage, and this is confirmed by some of the features of the dome itself: it was built of overlapping layers of wedges of tuff radiating outwards, with parts which sag and rectangular windows inserted at random in addition to the circular skylight at the apex, with no attempt to coordinate them with the structure or the decorative mosaic work. The next step in this architectural genre was the "**Tempio di Venere**", dating from the reign of Hadrian (117-138 AD). This rotunda stands on the waterfront, at present some 6.20 metres below ground level. Here too the weight of the dome is supported by a double wall in *opus latericium*, circular inside and octagonal outside, with the angles flanked by massive pilasters. Unlike the Tempio di Mercurio, here there is a rationale in the

apertures linking the exterior and interior, for the row of eight windows inserted above the load-bearing structure correspond to the eight segments of the exterior. These in turn characterise the space inside, and the result is a segmented vault, with sixteen segments alternating ribbed and spherical curvatures rising from above and between the window arches. The decoration too is more elaborate: whereas in the Tempio di Mercurio the marble facing was only taken up as far as the windowsills and there was mosaic work only inside the dome, here both the load-bearing wall and the outside of the dome were covered with chequers of white stucco interspersed with bands of blue glass paste, creating a striking effect particularly when seen from the sea. The overall effect was

enhanced by other buildings grouped around it, including a chamber with concave walls to the southwest, with three tiny round rooms built onto the convex walls; analogous to some structures in the Villa of Hadrian at Tivoli, this was probably a *calidarium*.

The original appearance of the Tempio di Venere, preserved in engravings, has been greatly altered both by the significant subsidence and by misconceived restoration carried out in the first part of the 20th century. Recent selective excavations have confirmed that it too was a *natatio* (pool), fed probably by mineral springs located along the seafront. It seems originally to have been part of what we know as the Sector of Venere at the foot of the hillside, for it was built opposite the rectangular hall with an apse.

It was only isolated when the coast road was constructed (now Via Lucullo). In his work *De Balnis Puteolanis,* Pietro da Eboli identifies this Roman bath as the Bagno di Bracula.

The culmination of the architectural learning curve in domed structures at Baia is the "**Tempio di Diana**", which gets its name from the discovery of a bas relief here featuring animals with a frieze invoking the goddess. It was erected as part of a programme of building works undertaken by Alexandrus Severus (208-235 AD) which included a palace and grandiose baths to commemorate his mother Julia Mamea. The decoration of the external load-bearing structure is here taken to new lengths with a scenographic design alternating large windows and lunettes typical of Roman taste

Tempio di Diana. This may have been part of the Imperial palace of Alexander Severus (208-235 AD)

Tempio di Diana,
ground-plan,
cross-section
and axonometric
reconstruction

Facing page:
Tempio di Diana
with the harbour
and castle of Baia
in the background

in this period. Again there is a circular interior and octagonal exterior in *opus caementicium*, and the monument is now below ground to the sills of the large windows, of which four out of eight survive, interspersed with segmented lunettes. The walls are faced in *opus mixtum* (two rows of brick and one of tuff blocks) up to the spring of the dome. In this case the structure was not buttressed at the crown of the dome, and in fact it collapsed; the building as a whole is characterised by inferior workmanship. The dome, half of which fell in, is hemispherical rather than ogival; its lower section is built in *opus vittatum* (alternating brick and tuff) and the upper part in irregular tuff blocks set in mortar and progressively protruding. It too was originally the main bathing room of a spa establishment, remains of which can still be seen around it. In medieval times it was known as the Bagno dei Gibborosi or "hunchbacks", on account of its peculiar shape. There is still a spring welling up to the south of this building, which is sandwiched between the railway and private houses and undergoing restoration.

The Archaeological Park and Monumental Park

The hillside overlooking the bay of Baia is entirely covered with the remains of buildings built on a series of terraces. The area that has been excavated from the 1920s onwards and open to the public, known as the Archaeological Park or Baths of Baia, covers some 40,000 square metres lying between two roads running along the brow of the hill, Via Sella di Baia and Via Bellavista, and another that cuts across the lower slopes, Via Lucullo. The rest of the hillside, occupying a further 150,000 square metres and called the Monumental Park, has recently been provided with a visitors' route and joined up with the Archaeological Park. Here too you can now inspect a series of highly important archaeological remains while enjoying a beautiful panorama and the luxuriant Mediterranean maquis.

The Archaeological Park
A glance at the map shows a series of residential buildings grouped in separate nuclei, which bear all the marks of having been constructed under imperial supervision: this was in all likelihood the *Palatium Baianum*, or at least part of it. The buildings continued to be used in one way or another up to medieval times, and even in some cases until the early 1900s. They have thus lost almost all their original decoration (schemes comprising marble facing, painting and stucco work). This nudity largely dispels their original splendour, but the impressive scale and sophistication of the surviving architecture does give some idea of it. Scholars have sought to give an identity to the endless succession of buildings by dividing the area into five sectors: Villa dell'Ambulatio, Mercurio, Sosandra, Venere and Piccole Terme. The buildings are located along the hillside, descending from the ridge on successive terraces so that each lower level functions as the substruction (foundation or support) for the building above it. This construction technique was an extension of that used in building the villas of the late Republican era involving artificial foundations (*basis villae*). Two commanding flights of steps serve to both link and distinguish the various levels of each sector. The map also clearly shows which sectors were built on the same orientation, indicating not only that they date from the same period but also, as we shall see, that they served similar purposes. Look for example at the Sectors of Sosandra (in yellow on the map on p. 32) and Villa dell'Ambulatio (in green). Both were

The Archaeological Park of Baia: some of the terraces of the Villa dell'Ambulatio, with the servants' quarters dating from the 1ˢᵗ century AD, restructured in the 4ᵗʰ century to provide accommodation for people using the baths

The Archaeological Park of Baia - Overall layout

VILLA DELL'AMBULATIO
end 2nd cent. B.C. - 3rd cent. A.D.

SECTOR OF MERCURIO
1st cent. B.C. - 3rd cent. A.D.

SECTOR OF SOSANDRA
end 2nd cent. B.C. - 2nd cent. A.D.

SECTOR OF VENERE
2nd cent. B.C. - 4th cent. A.D.

1 - **TERRACE A**: peristyle (1st cent. BC - 1
2 - **TERRACE C**: portico with pillars (1st
3 - **TERRACE D**: servants' quarters - *ho*
4 - **TERRACE E**: residential rooms (1st - 3
5 - **TERRACE F**: garden.
6 - **Baths** (1st cent. BC - 2nd cent. AD).
7 - **Tempio di Mercurio** (1st cent. BC).
8 - **Baths** (reign of Severus: 193-235 AD).
9 - **Hot spring with fumarole.**
10 - **Octagonal room** (reign of Severus: 193
11 - **Corridor with archway** (early 1st cent.
12 - **Quadriporticus** ("piscina") (1st - 2nd ce
13 - **Wall paintings** (1st - 2nd cent. AD).

← **ROUTE FOR VISITORS**

Ⅰ Ⅱ Ⅲ Ⅳ Ⅴ Ⅵ
INFORMATION PANELS

st cent. AD).

st - 3rd cent. AD).

).

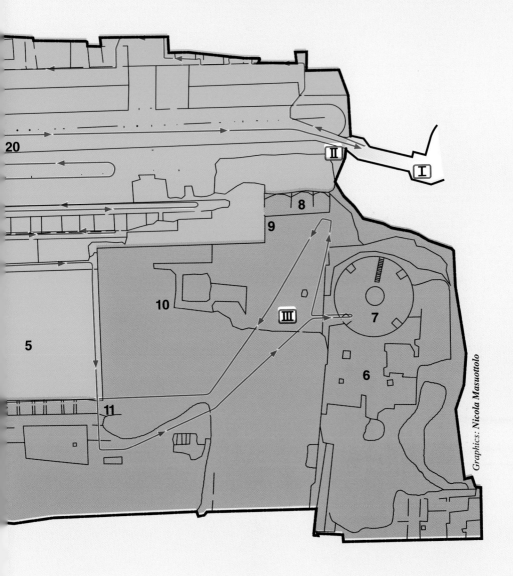

Graphics: Nicola Masuottolo

originally developed in the 2nd and 1st century BC with walls built in *opus incertum* (now below ground, not visible). Such walls were presumably what remained of villas already standing here, incorporated into the new constructions. The present layout of both these sectors dates from the first years of the Christian era and resembles the typical disposition of a villa with terraces and porticoes, quite conventional in the latter sector, more articulated and with modifications in the former.

The **Sector of the Villa dell'Ambulatio** is laid out on six terraces, the first three of which display a coherent overall design. The highest terrace, A, is occupied by the domestic quarters, with the peristyle (1), living rooms and cubiculi opening off a large main room (*oecus*) overlooking the bay. The flooring throughout was originally decorated either with marble (*opus sectile*) or in black and white mosaic. At first terrace B merely shored up the buildings above, but it was soon provided with a double curtain-wall in *opus reticulatum* and turned into a covered walkway (*ambulatio*) (20), from which the sector gets its name. It is divided down the middle with a row of pillars and linking

Statue known as Aspasia (actually Aphrodite Sosandra), found in the Terme di Baia. Naples, National Archaeological Museum

arches, and has a large central room situated beneath the one on the terrace above. The same layout (portico and central panoramic room) is reproduced on terrace C, while the lower levels have undergone radical modifications. The servants' quarters on terrace D (3), dating from the 1st century AD, were evidently restructured much later (perhaps in the 4th century), probably for use as *hospitalia*, accommodation for people using the nearby baths (in the sectors of Mercurio, Venere and Piccole Terme). This obviously came about after the imperial era, when this complex passed into public ownership. Terrace E was also substantially modified: built originally with a series of blind arches and semicolumns, it was subsequently incorporated into rooms built below (4). The lowest level (F) was seriously damaged in post-Roman times by people searching for underwater springs; it was occupied by a large garden (5), bounded to the west by the long containing wall of the level above. The garden may originally have been surrounded by a portico, for remains of wall paintings in the III style are to be seen in the south-west corner.

The **Sector of Sosandra** (in yellow), comprising the central segment of the whole complex, features four phases of construction between the mid-1st century BC and the 2nd century AD. It is laid out on four levels, once again with the residential quarters on the upper two levels. The top terrace is occupied by service rooms, and the next one down has dining and living rooms and also a small steam bath (*laconicum*) with stucco decorations, overlooking the bay and preceded by a colonnade (17). All these rooms were very well appointed, with mosaic flooring, notably one dating

from the 2nd century AD adorned
with actors' masks and with a
centrepiece featuring a theatrical
scene, and also sculptures. In the
largest room (18), the statue known
first as Aspasia and subsequently as
Aphrodite Sosandra stood in the
central recess in the rear wall. The
original was in bronze in the late-
Severe style, attributed to Kalamis, an
Athenian sculptor active in the early
5th century BC; this copy in Parian
marble was made during the reign of
Hadrian. In the room next door stood
a statue of Hermes; the head was
stolen but subsequently retrieved and
is now in the National Archaeological
Museum of Naples, as is the
Aphrodite Sosandra. Both sculptures
were produced in a workshop of
copyists that catered for commissions
from the imperial household from the
Augustan era until the last years of
the reign of Hadrian. The workshop
was certainly located in Baia, possibly
on the premises of the imperial

residence. In 1954, during work to
consolidate the substruction of this
terrace, archaeologists found a
deposit of discarded fragments of
plaster sculptures used as moulds for
making copies. These are now
displayed in one of the rooms of the
Archaeological Museum of the
Phlegraean Fields.
The lower two levels are completely
different in character. They are
occupied by a very striking
architectonic ensemble, with a
semicircular edifice up above (14)
and below it a large open-air site
traditionally known as the *piscina*
(12). The former resembles a theatre
with a terrace instead of the stands
(*cavea*), a round pool in the middle
of the orchestra and an architectonic
façade with alcoves and columns. It
seems to have been a theatre-
nymphaeum, used for spectacles
based on marine subjects complete
with water features and waterfalls.
As for the piscina, there is nothing to

*The Archaeological
Park of Baia: general
view of the Sector
of Sosandra.
In the foreground the
theatre-nymphaeum*

suggest that it was used for bathing, although the area has never been excavated down to the foundations, lying some 6 metres below the present ground level. It might perhaps have been the *ebeterion* (place of recreation for youths) that the historian Cassius Dio records Nero having built in Baia for the sailors stationed at Misenum. In fact the layout recalls the complex at Pompeii comprising the Theatre and the Palaestra of the Gladiators: this area may have served the same purpose, with the added attraction of a plentiful water supply, exploited in fountains and waterfalls both in the open air and below ground. The room at the centre of the portico beneath lies on the same axis as the semicircular pool of the theatre-nymphaeum (14) and another

chamber hollowed out of the cliff behind it. Here too there is ample evidence of transformations made after the restructuring carried out in the 2nd century AD. In the portico of the piscina a series of rooms were

analogous to those carried out in the Villa dell'Ambulatio. Here too, then, they probably date from the 4th century AD, when the emperors lost interest in Baia and the Phlegraean Fields. This was partly on account of the effects of bradyseism and partly because the emperors themselves were much more involved with provinces outside the Italian peninsula. Thus the structures in Baia were adapted for other uses, particularly as accommodation for people coming to take the waters. In one of the rooms opening off the western portico of the piscina, now lying below ground level and partially under water, there are the same stone tanks found in two rooms of the baths next to the Tempio di Mercurio. This also seems to have been a venue for therapeutic baths in medieval times, and can probably be identified as the "Baths of the Fairies" recorded by Pietro da Eboli in *De Balneis*. This spring continued to be exploited until quite recently, being known as the "scabies water" since it was beneficial for skin conditions.
In presenting the remaining sectors, we shall limit ourselves to describing some of the main features: they all comprise bathing establishments which remained in use up until the Middle Ages, and we have already seen the construction and purpose of the three large "temples".
The **Sector of Mercurio** (in orange) takes its name from the Tempio di Mercurio. It comprises two groups of buildings, prevalently for bathing, situated to the north-east (6) and the south-west (10). We know little about the former because the buildings lie below ground with water up to the level of the vaults; moreover various parts were destroyed when new housing was put up and during construction of the road along the

The Archaeological Park of Baia: Sector of Venere and Tempio di Venere, aerial view. The unity of the original spa complex has been disrupted by the modern road

Below:
The Archaeological Park of Baia: Sector of Venere, the large nymphaeum with apse in the baths dating from the reign of Hadrian

created by the rather clumsy insertion of long partition walls, and the space inside the nymphaeum was similarly divided up. We cannot be sure when these modifications were made, but at least in the portico they seem to be

north-east of the site. Structures in *opus reticulatum* indicate that there were already buildings here in the late Republican or early Imperial era, subsequently restructured in *opus latericium* during the 2nd century AD. In one of these rooms the fine head of the Omphalos Apollo in Pentelic marble was found, also a copy of a Greek bronze in the late-Severe style like the Aspasia and Hermes found in the Sector of Sosandra, all made in the same local workshop. The group of buildings to the south-west, on the other hand, were all put up during the Severus reigns, as we can tell from the use of red brickwork. These were particularly sumptuous premises in terms of both design, as in the octagonal room with dome and wall recesses (10), and decoration, with elaborate wall paintings and relief stucco work. It could in fact have been part of Alexander Severus's palace, which would have extended down to the shoreline, where during the 1920s various architectonic fragments dating from his reign were found in the sea.

The **Sector of Venere** (in blue) gets its name from the "rooms of Venus", as they were called by eighteenth century scholars. These are three rooms on the lower level (14b) adorned with fine stucco work on the ceilings in the manner of boudoirs. The sector comprises three groups of buildings dating from different periods on the lower, intermediate and upper levels, the latter known as the Piccole Terme. The eastern side of the lower level (A) was completely disrupted by construction of the coast road (Via Lucullo) with modern buildings along it, leaving the large bath house, the Tempio di Venere, sticking out like a sore thumb. The development on this level, clearly a separate entity with respect to the

levels above since it has a different orientation, comprises two groups of buildings standing on the western side of a large uncovered area, only partially excavated, which was probably a garden. Along the northern side there are a fountain, a small room with a female herm in the centre and a mosaic featuring a cherub with a baby hare, possibly representing Autumn, and an exedra or summer dining-room, all dating from the 2nd century AD. The succession of rooms on the western side date from two different periods. To the north there are three chambers (the so-called rooms of Venus) originally used for bathing and dating from the beginning of the 1st century AD (14b). The scant remains of stucco work in bas relief on the ceiling have been thoroughly blackened by the torches wielded by travellers on the Grand Tour; moreover, these rooms were inhabited for a long period. The stucco work featured subjects drawn from the palaestra and the baths – wrestlers, nymphs, sea creatures and swans – as we know from drawings made by Francesco Bartoli in the years 1700-1724 (now conserved at Eton College). This decoration can be dated to the middle years of the 1st century AD. Subsequently the rooms were turned into water tanks and service rooms, including a kitchen with a cooking range and sinks. The buildings at the southern end of the western side constitute a large bathing establishment built during the reign of Hadrian. It is arranged round a large rectangular hall with an apse at the centre of the lower level (A), roofed with half-dome vaults and perfectly aligned with the Tempio di Venere. It is entirely occupied by a basin filled from fountains and water jets, probably a nymphaeum, with on either side two large rooms with a Greek cross ground-plan, roofed with cross vaulting.

This large complex, built at the same time as the radical transformation carried out in the adjacent Sector of Sosandra (see above), was probably used by the emperor Hadrian. He is known to have spent long periods in Baia, and he died here in 138 AD. Furthermore, it was during his reign, as Carlo Gasparri has established, that the repertoire of the local workshop of sculptors was renewed, taking as models Greek works in the late-Severe style dating from the 5th century BC (Aspasia, Hermes, Omphalos Apollo). This corresponded to the idealised conception held by Hadrian of Athenian civilisation between the end of the Persian wars and the age of Pericles.

An impressive ramp of broad steps along the north side of the Sector of Venere led up to the intermediate level (15, closed to the public), comprising an artificial terrace supported by robust vaults filling in the large gap between the lower and upper levels. On account of its very poor state of conservation, this terrace has remained largely uninvestigated. The buildings date from the 1st-4th century AD, and comprise a double row of service and store rooms, leading to an octagonal chamber (B), probably a bath house, aligned with the *laconicum* above it. Built above these rooms there was a baths suite (C) whose individual

The Archaeological Park of Baia: ground-plan of the last phase of the Minor Baths

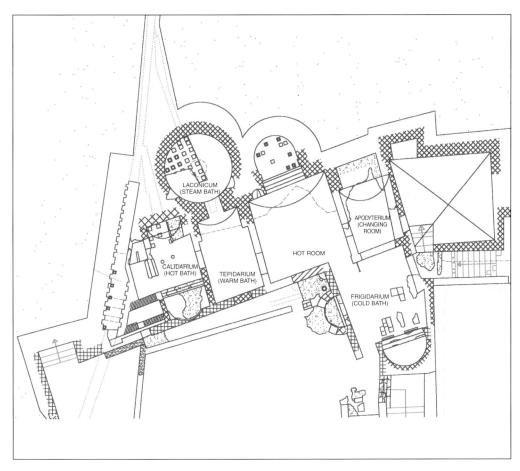

The Monumental Park: the "Villa of Julius Caesar". The oldest section (3rd-2nd century BC) built from large blocks of tuff

The Monumental Park: the "Villa of Julius Caesar". The portico on the crest of the hill which overlooks the bays below, as recorded by Tacitus in the Annales

rooms caved in and are now virtually unrecognisable. The unheated rooms lay to the north, including the *frigidarium* with its wall recesses and central pool; to the south the remains of *suspensurae* indicate the heated rooms, with an octagonal *laconicum*. In the courtyard in front of the suite we can identify other service rooms and a ramp leading down to a large underground room, also probably used for bathing, now inaccessible. The so-called **Piccole Terme** (Minor Baths, 16, closed to the public), are built on two levels and occupy the upper western side of this level, standing against the hillside. They exploit the hot springs inside the hill by means of tunnels. This is one of the oldest examples of baths suites known to us: the original structure, dating from the middle of the 1st century BC, comprised simply a rotunda in *opus reticulatum* (a prototype for all future baths), where bathers would take the *sudatio* (dry steam bath), and a pool of cold water, *frigidarium*. This structure was probably part of a villa dating from the late-Republican period, of which more remains may well come to light during excavations above and below these remains. Further bathing facilities were added over the next 100 years, including the *calidarium* and *tepidarium* built opposite the *laconicum*, probably when the baths were opened to the public. In the final phase (see plan on p. 39), dating from the 2nd century AD, the original *frigidarium* was turned into another heated room, and a larger cold room was built on the north-east side of the courtyard, provided with two pools. To the south, water tanks were added and a long channel was cut into the hillside to convey hot vapour to the baths. In the area to the north, still awaiting excavation, two colossal statues were found representing the heavenly twins, Castor and Pollux. They are copies in Pentelic marble based on originals by Polycletes, active in Athens in the mid-5th century BC, produced in the local workshop in the mid-2nd century AD. They are now on display in the National Archaeological Museum of Naples.

Monumental Park:
The "Villa of Julius Caesar"

This area is a continuation of the hillside with the remains of the Palatium, covering some 14 hectares and acquired by the state in 1936. Since September 1998 visitors have been able to enter this park from Via Bellavista and appreciate both the remains of this villa and the wonderful views over the bays of Baia on one side and Cuma on the other. A path through the luxuriant Mediterranean maquis brings you to the Archaeological Park. Excavations carried out on the summit of this area have revealed a large Roman villa, of which only the oldest core of buildings has so far been exposed. It is possible to distinguish four main phases of construction, going from the early 2nd century BC through to at least the 3rd century AD.

Phase I (in red)

The earliest structures are built in pseudo-polygonal style, with large blocks of tuff set in a loamy mortar. The western-most section of wall exposed runs northwards, and may have constituted a ramp. Two courses of rough-hewn blocks were incorporated into a subsequent construction and are all that is left of the original walls. Down at floor level, a patch of which has survived, there is a row of small arches, probably designed to let water drain off, which were blocked up at a later date. These structures seem to be all that was left standing of foundations (*basis villae*) dating back at least to the 2nd century BC.

Phase II (in beige)

To judge from stratigraphic evidence, the first villa on this site appears to have been destroyed by fire. It was

Wall painting in the late II style, found in the Monumental Park, the "Villa of Julius Caesar"

The Monumental Park of Baia

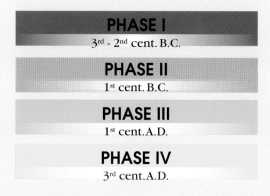

PHASE I
3rd - 2nd cent. B.C.

PHASE II
1st cent. B.C.

PHASE III
1st cent. A.D.

PHASE IV
3rd cent. A.D.

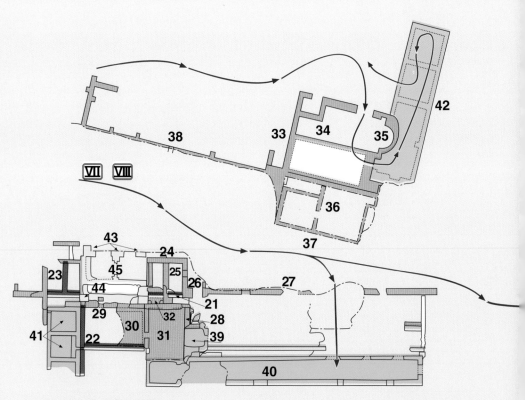

Graphics: Nicola Masuottolo

ROMAN VILLA. 3rd - 2nd cent. BC

21-23 : remains of base in pseudo-polygonal style.

24-25 : containing walls added between phases I and II.

ROMAN VILLA ATTRIBUTED TO JULIUS CAESAR. 1st cent. BC

26-29 : rooms and extended portico in *opus reticulatum*.

30-32 : remains of flooring.

33-38 : rooms in *opus reticulatum*.

TRANSFORMATION OF VILLA. 1st cent. AD

39-42 : water tanks in *opus caementicium* lined with *cocciopesto*.

ENLARGEMENT OF BUILDING. Probably during Severus reign (193 - 235 AD)

43-45 : vaulted rooms; pilasters in *opus latericium*.

ROUTE FOR VISITORS

VII   VIII

INFORMATION PANELS

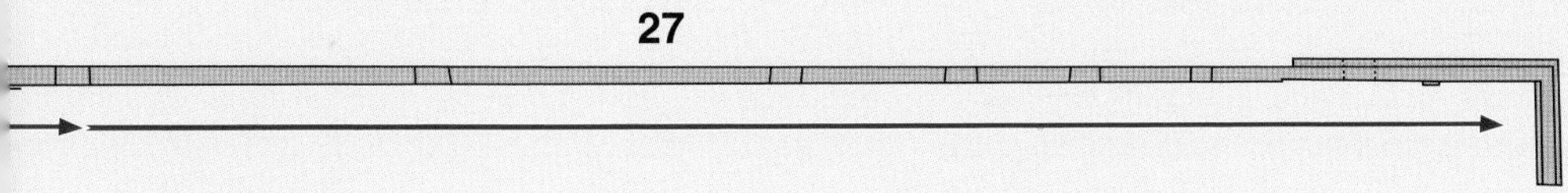

27

replaced by a much larger one which extended at least 150 metres northwards along the ridge and down the western face of the hillside with two rows of buildings on successive terraces, and probably over the eastern face as well. Investigation of this villa has only just begun. Its construction technique was *opus quasi reticulatum* using regular tuff blocks (*cubilia*). Above the original villa there were rooms, in one of which the flooring has been conserved. It comprises a layer of off-white mortar with slips of multi-coloured marble and vase necks set into it, and also traces of marble slabs. The sector of the villa extending northwards comprises a wall 139 metres long, with another wall closing it off at right-angles, both in *opus reticulatum*. There are traces of plaster painted in the II style along the interior of this wall, and openings for doors and windows, some splayed on the east-facing side. This seems to indicate a portico built overlooking the bay of Baia, and there is further evidence for this in a deposit of tiles that had fallen from a roof, found in a test excavation. On the western face of the hillside the remains of at least two rows of buildings in *opus reticulatum* with vaulted ceilings are aligned north-south, suggesting that terraces had once been built along the contours of the hillside. The villa also extended over the eastern side: the upper part collapsed in a landslip, but there are remains conserved lower down. A fragment of fresco, decorated when the so-called II style of wall-painting was evolving into the III style (circa 30-10 BC), was found here but removed to ensure its preservation.

Phase III (in blue)

During this phase the earlier structures were modified and a series of water tanks constructed (only partially excavated) to the north, east and south, the largest of which stood above ground. This still conserves part of the walls and the vaulted roof, the facing in *signinum* (crushed terracotta with mosaic tesserae inserted) and a curb at the base.

Phase IV (in yellow)

This is an extension of the rooms on the western side. There are remains of containing walls in *opus caementicium* and two vaulted chambers with a platform built above them, supporting two brick pillars. These structures probably date from the Severus reigns, as do the remains of some thick flooring which had collapsed, suggesting the existence of a substantial construction.

The panoramic location of this edifice and the remains of wall paintings dating back to the 2nd century BC (Phase I) indicate that it was a residential complex. In the mid-1st century BC it was turned into a spacious villa, with terracing down both slopes of the hillside, overlooking the bays of Baia and Cuma. In 1890 Beloch indicated this stretch of coastline, to the west of the Aragonese Castle, as the location of the villa of Julius Caesar on the basis of literary sources. Tacitus, in the *Annales* XIV 9.3, describes its situation *quae subiectos sinus editissima prospecta* ("which from the highest point overlooks the bays below"), while Cicero, in *Ad Atticum* XII, 40, locates it *in regione Baiana … summis iugis montium* ("in the region of Baia … on the crest of the hill"). In view of its dating, mid-1st century BC, panoramic position, exceptional size and the presence of structures and decorations dating from the 1st century BC, it seems highly probable that this was indeed the villa of Julius Caesar.

The Aragonese Castle: the Archaeological Museum of the Phlegraean Fields

The Castle

This fine monument occupies a commanding position on the headland to the south of the bay of Baia. The ramp leading up to it was built above the original flight of broad steps leading to a drawbridge. This was replaced early on by a large gateway in volcanic piperno, subsequently adorned with the Bourbon coat of arms. The castle as we see it today broadly corresponds to the design adopted during its restructuring by the Viceroy Pedro di Toledo, with successive alterations and additions. It was built on top of the ruins of a Roman villa, traditionally ascribed to Julius Caesar (but see the latest findings, presented in the previous chapter). In fact it was probably part of Nero's residence. As we saw above (page 13), the caption *stagnum Neronis* on the glass flasks from Puteoli may refer to the fishpools lying just off the castle. The extant remains show that the villa, built on various levels, occupied the crest of the headland, where the Padiglione Cavaliere now stands, and extended along the eastern side. Here there are remains of a vaulted ramp hewn out of the cliff, faced in *opus reticulatum* with wall paintings, which zigzagged

down to the shore below. This part of the hillside is covered with ancient remains that have always stood exposed. They include water tanks and rooms belonging to bath suites at different levels, right down to the shore, where the large fishpools are now under water. When restoration began recently on the Padiglione Cavaliere, which incorporated the Roman *domus*, a significant discovery was made. The villa was built on at least two levels, the lower one being older, in *opus reticulatum*, and the upper one in *opus mixtum* (interspersed with brick courses). Both levels were conserved when the Aragonese erected the bastion: the chambers of the lower level were simply reused, with very little structural

Mosaic flooring overlying flooring in signinum, *from the Roman villa beneath the Padiglione Cavaliere in the castle of Baia*

Following pages: *the castle of Baia*

Overall layout of the castle of Baia

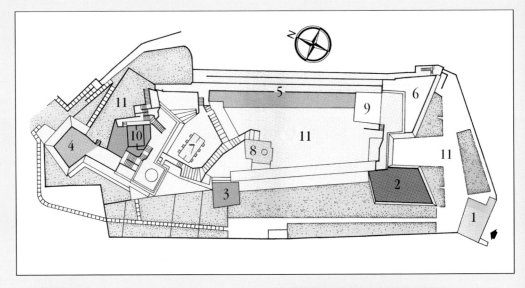

1. Gatehouse.
2. Mezzaluna block.
3. Blockhouse.
4. North West Tower or Torre Tenaglia.
5. Dormitory wing, to be incorporated in the museum
6. Former prison cells.

7. Powder magazine of Sant'Antonio.
8. 16th century chapel.
9. Former barracks.
10. Padiglione Cavaliere, officers' quarters.
11. Parade ground and courtyards.

integration, while the curtain walls were built on top of the upper level, duly reinforced. Even the mosaic floors of the Roman *domus* have been conserved: the technique of the mosaic work, *tessellatum,* dates them to the Julio-Claudian era, and in one case this overlays an earlier flooring in *signinum*. Once excavation work has been finished, visitors will be able to view all the phases of the castle's history, from the remains of the Roman villa to the fortifications of the Aragonese period and up to the present day. The first castle to be erected on this site was commissioned by the Aragonese King of Naples Alfonso II, as part of a system of defences for the kingdom built in the years 1490-93. The castle was designed to guard the approach to Pozzuoli, where an enemy landing would have threatened to outflank the main defences of the city of Naples. The man put in charge of its construction was Francesco di Giorgio Martini, a native of Siena, who was an architect, engineer and artist, and the leading expert of the age in defensive structures (notably towers and tunnels) and war machinery. He was probably responsible for the construction of the North West Tower crowned with battlements (Torre Tenaglia). It had an arsenal on the lower level and powder magazine above it. Beneath the tower galleries were lined with barrels of gunpowder to be exploded in case of withdrawal, as in other castles built by Martini at Montefeltro.

The castle was radically altered following the eruption which produced Monte Nuovo in 1538. The Spanish Viceroy, Pedro di Toledo, implemented the design we see today, with a double curtain wall with battlements. There was also a moat protecting the southern approach, the only side which lacked the natural protection of a sheer cliff face, filled in in 1927. Two square emplacements were built for the first and second batteries of Sant'Antonio at the southern corner, separated by the courtyard of the Mezzaluna. There were also the two batteries of the Cavaliere, covering the western approach, one sea battery and five draw-bridges, all subsequently rebuilt in stone. Various outbuildings were added by successive viceroys: the Padiglione Cavaliere, dominating the castle at its northern end (and incorporating the Roman villa), containing the quarters of the commander and officers of the garrison; the prison cells, with inmates' graffiti still visible on the walls; the powder magazine of Sant'Antonio; and the chapel, with the chaplain's lodging next door. The chapel, built in 1556, is known as the "Madonna del Pilar" after the late-16th century altarpiece, currently undergoing restoration at the Museum of Capodimonte. Two other paintings from the same period, "Saint Barbara with the Baptist" and "Saint Rocco and the Madonna of the Rosary and Saints" adorned the side altars. During the chapel's restoration they are displayed on the staircase of the North West Tower.

With the end of Bourbon rule in Naples (1734-1860) the castle went into an inexorable decline. It was occupied by the Royal Military Orphanage from 1927 to 1975, and during this period it was substantially altered, with original structures being knocked down or walled in. Following the earthquake in 1980 it gave temporary

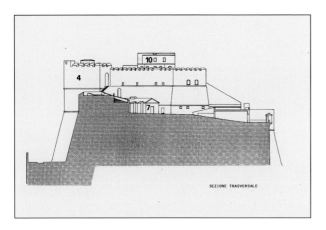

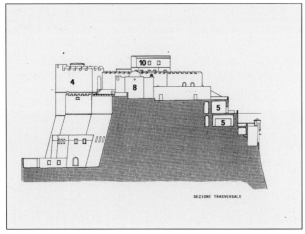

The castle of Baia, cross-section of the Tower (4), Padiglione Cavaliere (10) and Powder Magazine (7)

The castle of Baia, cross-section of the Tower (4), chapel (8), Padiglione Cavaliere (10) and rooms of the former Refectory (5)

accommodation to people left homeless, and again suffered considerable damage. It was largely derelict when in 1984 it was assigned to the Soprintendenza Archeologica in Naples. A plan was drawn up for its refurbishment and use, and restoration work began, in collaboration with the Soprintendenza ai Beni Ambientali ed Architettonici. The first phase of restoration involved four sectors: the North West Tower, presenting an initial display of material belonging to the Archaeological Museum of the Phlegraean Fields; the section of the curtain wall along the path leading to this tower; the parapet walk leading from the Torre Tenaglia round the north and east

sides as far as the second draw-bridge; and the lower level of the battery of Sant'Antonio, restructured as an auditorium. Work is currently in progress on the rooms of the former refectory, on two levels, destined for topographical displays of archaeological contexts found locally both on land and in the sea, and a section of paintings featuring the Phlegraean Fields.

The Archaeological Museum of the Phlegraean Fields

The museum was inaugurated in 1993 in the North West Tower. The courtyard leading to the tower displays the marble plinths found in the Sacellum of the Augustals. The first floor presents a life-size reconstruction of the architectonic and sculptural decoration of this shrine. On the second floor there is an imaginative display of all the material recovered from the nymphaeum of Punta Epitaffio. The museum's collections include a range of plaster casts from Baia, on display next to the auditorium on the route from the castle entrance to the North West Tower (Corpo della Mezzaluna). Once restoration work has been completed, the rest of the museum's collections will be on view in the 44 rooms of the former refectory, occupying two levels on the north-eastern side of the castle. The following description takes you on a tour of the current exhibits starting from the castle entrance.

Room of the "plaster casts from Baia"

During the excavation of a small room in the so-called Baths of Sosandra in 1954, archaeologists came across hundreds of fragments of plasterwork. They proved to be

Interior of the chapel in the castle of Baia, with the altarpiece of the Madonna del Pilar, currently being restored at the Museum of Capodimonte

the discards of a local sculptors' workshop, the first tangible proof of such a centre of production in Baia. It carried out commissions for the imperial household, from the last years of the 1st century BC through to the 2nd century AD, and must have been situated either within the household or nearby.

Local craftsmen produced copies in marble of masterpieces of classical and Hellenistic art by taking plaster casts from the bronze originals. These fragments were discarded in post-Roman times, when the workshop was no longer active. Various products of the workshop came to light in Baia, notably the statues of Aspasia, Hermes, the Omphalos Apollo and the head of the Mattei Amazon. Two scholars, Hans Schuchardt and Christa Landwehr, undertook a systematic study of the fragments, and succeeded in attributing some sixty of them to Greek originals, all lost and known to us only from Roman copies. In only one case did a fragment reproduce a face, identified as Aristogites from the group of the Tyrannicides. The scholars carried out their quest by fitting the fragments into modern casts taken from the surviving sculptures: the technique is exemplified using the statue known as Narcissus.

*"Hera Borghese",
in the Room
of the Plaster Casts
in the Museum*

The showcases contain the fragments recognised on the basis of Roman copies and identified with the following Greek originals: *1-2* Group of the Tyrannicides, Armodios and Aristogites (circa 490 BC); *3* Persephone of Corinth (mid-5th century BC); *4-6* Amazons of Ephesus: Amazon of Sosikles, Sciarra and Mattei (440-430 BC); *7* Aphrodite, known as Hera Borghese (circa 420 BC); *8* Athena of Velletri (circa 420-410 BC); *9* Westmacott Ephebe (late 5th century BC); *10* so-called Narcissus (late 5th century BC) with a modern copy made by the Skulpturhalle, Basle; *11* Belvedere Apollo (circa 330 BC); *12* Plutos (360 BC). *13* an assortment of fragments (heads, hands, feet, drapery) which, in spite of being well conserved and clearly Greek, have not been identified, perhaps because no Roman copies of the original have come down to us. *14* statue of Aphrodite, one of three examples found in Baia, in the pose known as the Hera Borghese. The other two are in the National Archaeological Museum of Naples; this one was found in the sea off Miseno in 1980, and is on view for the first time. We know for certain that these copies were produced in the local workshop thanks to the discovery among the plaster fragments of a piece from the goddess's very delicate robe (7).

**Courtyard of the Plinths
from the Sacellum of the Augustals**
(see plan on pp. 78-79)
The Augustals were the priests charged with celebrating the cult of the Emperor. Eleven plinths bearing inscriptions have been set up in the

courtyard leading to the Tower. They were originally surmounted by statues featuring the emperors who were worshipped in the shrine, and also gods and prominent Augustals. The statues stood in a courtyard in front of the sacellum itself, and were probably arrayed according to hierarchy, with those of the Augustals standing to one side. All the plinths are made of marble apart from one in brick (plinth 9), from which a slab from the facing is on display. They all bear inscriptions, with the exception of plinth 7, telling us a lot about the cult. The dedicatee is named on the front, together with the names of the dedicants; on the sides appear the date of the dedication, the motivations and often the entire text of the Augustals' resolution. Thus we have information about the workings of the college, the wealth of its members and the granting of large sums for public works. This would presumably have secured privileges and social prestige for the members of the college. The bas reliefs which feature on some of the plinths are also very informative. On the largest, dedicated to Trajan (plinth 1), there are representations of the divinity who watched over the imperial fleet (*tutela classis)* and the Genius of the colony. These two figures can be identified from the inscription on plinth 9, which records that statues of them stood in the forum of Misenum. Plinth 4 has bas reliefs of two two-masted cargo ships. The earliest dedications refer to the reigns of Nerva and Trajan (96-117 AD); after a gap during the reigns of Hadrian and Antoninus Pius, others refer to Marcus Aurelius and Lucius Verus (161-169 AD). The earliest period of the shrine is also recorded in an inscription honouring Domitian, subsequently reused for Vespasian, but we have no inscriptions dating from the founding of the cult in the early years of the Imperial period.

Room of the Sacellum of the Augustals: the temple and its sculptures

This is a reconstruction of the architectonic features and sculptures recovered from the Sacellum of the Augustals at Misenum. The

Fragment of the head of Aristotigones, in the Room of the Plaster Casts in the Museum

Marble plinth from the Sacellum of the Augustals: detail of the bas relief showing the divinity who watched over the Imperial fleet at Miseno

Room of the Sacellum of the Augustals. Reconstruction of the façade of the temple. Inside, portrait-statues of Vespasian and Titus; on the right, bronze equestrian statue of Domitian-Nerva

monument was discovered in 1968 on the site of the forum, facing the sea, and now lies underwater as a result of bradyseism. The parts investigated so far are the main temple, dedicated to Augustus and the Genius of the Augustals, and the area reserved for the priests, opening off a portico. The eleven plinths once surmounted by statues of emperors, divinities and leading priests were found inside this portico. The shrine dates back to the Augustan era, with evidence of subsequent refurbishings. It was radically rebuilt in the second half of the 2nd century AD, and destroyed in an earthquake soon afterwards.

The layout recreates its appearance following the major face-lift carried out in the second half of the 2nd century AD. Rising to nearly 7 metres in height, it incorporates all the original elements retrieved from the site. The façade of the tetrastyle pronaos with two columns in cipollino marble (the other two, together with all the capitals, were removed following its abandonment) is surmounted by a marble epistyle bearing the dedication of Lucius Lecanius

Sacellum of the Augustals, portrait-statue of Titus

Primitivus and Cassia Victoria. This couple financed the rebuilding work, and their portraits feature in the pediment. As dean of the Augustals, the husband dedicated a statue to Dionysus in 161 AD. He served as dean again in 165 (see inscriptions on plinths 4 and 11), and during these years the tempietto was rebuilt, which may have secured his wife's admission to the college, for she appears as the first dedicant in the relevant inscription. In the portraits the man's head is modelled on the official portrait of Antoninus Pius and the couple are surrounded by an oak wreath borne up by two Victories, in a typical example of self-exaltation. The corners of the pediment feature a dolphin, on the left, and a ship's prow on the right. Behind the pronaos, as if within the temple itself, stand the statues of Vespasian and Titus depicted in the style of heroic nudity. These would originally have stood inside the cella in two apses, flanking the inscription which identified the monument and which is still *in situ* (substituted here by a plaster cast). The inscription on the plinth of the statue of Vespasian reused in part a previous dedication to Domitian who, having incurred the *damnatio memoriae*, was eliminated from all monuments and records. The equestrian statue in bronze was also created to commemorate Domitian (81-96 AD) and re-dedicated to his successor Nerva (96-98 AD), with only the face being substituted. This statue was found in pieces in a room next to the temple. It can be dated to the final years of Domitian's reign, on the basis of the hair style, which also characterises the coinage from these years. The emperor is shown as a victorious military leader on a rearing horse. Few equestrian statues in bronze have come down to us, and this is the only one in such a dramatic pose: that of Marcus Aurelius in Rome shows the emperor astride a standing horse. Domitian is seen in the act of hurling a javelin, as in the sculpture of Alexander the Great done by Lysippus in 334 BC, which seems to have been the model for the smaller version known as "Alexander on horseback" found in Herculaneum and now in the National Archaeological Museum of Naples. The decoration of the cuirass is magnificent, involving

both raised and incised ornamentation and damascened work (using bronze and silver). It features the *gorgoneion*, alluding to Minerva, Hercules strangling the snakes, and sea creatures evoking the port of Misenum. Also on view are a high quality headless female statue in a pose characteristic of the early Imperial period known as the "Piccola Ercolanese", the goddess Fortune, and a slab from the facing of plinth 9 showing Oceanus, lying back with a tiller in his hand and observing the chariot of Helios. These statues date from the Severus reigns and document the continuing activity of the college of the Augustals during a period for which we have no epigraphic evidence.

Room of the Nymphaeum of Punta Epitaffio

This room gives you the feeling of entering the nymphaeum created for the emperor Claudius. For an accurate reconstruction of the site, see the scale model on display. In 1969 the tops of two marble statues were observed on the seabed, and found to be standing in a semicircular apse. They were of very high quality, and although the heads had been disfigured by stone-boring mussels, they could be identified as Ulysees and one of his companions. Ulysees was depicted holding out a drinking vessel, looking just like a silver bowl, while his companion is pouring wine from a wineskin. This apse must thus have recreated the scene from the Odyssey in which

Sacellum of the Augustals, detail of portrait-statue of Vespasian

Sacellum of the Augustals, detail of equestrian statue of Domitian-Nerva

Draped female statue known as the "Little girl from Herculaneum"

Statue of the goddess Fortune

Polyphemus is made drunk so that his captives can escape from his cave. Divers searching for the statue of the cyclops uncovered the full extent of the site, identified as a nymphaeum. It was a rectangular chamber, built on a lower level than the adjacent constructions at the foot of the hill as a realistic grotto. There was an exedra at one end, four recesses in each of the side walls and a large brickwork entrance gateway.

Statues would have stood in all the recesses: those in three from the eastern side and one from the western side have come down to us. The latter has been identified with certainty by Bernard Andreae as Claudius's mother, Antonia Augusta or Minor, on the basis of coins and portraits. She was the niece of Augustus, and deified during her son's reign (41-46 AD). In this sculpture, made after her death, the smooth skin of the face is in marked contrast to her hair and the crown of precious stones on her brow. In her left arm she is supporting a youth, with cavities in the back for metal wings to be inserted. This brings to mind Eros, suggesting that Antonia was depicted as *Venus genetrix*, although Marcello Gigante favours a different hypothesis: the fact that the youth had his feet crossed would make him an emblem of death (*thanatos*), indicating that Antonia herself was dead.

The statue from the first recess on the right represents a youthful, smiling Dionysus, in the sort of loose-limbed pose popularised by Praxiteles, playing with a panther, his sacred animal. In the second recess stood the statue of a girl with a melancholy air, whose physiognomy and hairstyle recall the portraits of children of the Julio-Claudian dynasty. Fausto Zevi has ascribed this figure to a funerary typology adopted throughout the 1st century AD for girls who died at an early age. He also maintains that the fragment of a hand with a butterfly belongs to this statue, in which case the child is portrayed at the moment in which life departs, the butterfly or *psyche* being a standard motif in Greek and Roman symbolism. In this case the statue would not be of

Claudia Octavia, the wife of Nero whom he had assassinated on Ventotene, but rather of one of Claudius's daughters who died in childhood. In the fourth recess there was another statue of Dionysus as a youth, shown here with pensive mien, crowned with ivy. Thus the nymphaeum was adorned with statues of two deceased members of Claudius's family and two representations of Dionysus. The whole nymphaeum has a Dionysiac aura, for the scene of Ulysses outwitting the Cyclops is a metaphor for the triumph of life over death, and the statues of Antonia and the girl seem to evoke their regeneration in the after-life. Five of the imperial nymphaea known to us feature the myth of Polyphemus: those of Tiberius at Sperlonga, Claudius at Baia, Nero in the Domus Aurea, Domitian at Castelgandolfo and Hadrian at

Tivoli. This mythical topic was particularly appropriate because it was possible to evoke the Dionysiac world and celebrate the potency of wine while at the same time depicting the punishment of the impious monster for imbibing in the sanctuary of the semi-divine nymphs.

The four missing statues may have been removed when the nymphaeum was abandoned. Bernard Andreae suggests that the lower part of a male sculpture should be identified as Drusus, Claudius's father, but the circumstances of its discovery exclude it from belonging to the context of the nymphaeum. His conjectural restitution of the missing sculptures as, on the left, Claudius's forebears (Augustus, his wife Livia and Drusus), and on the right Britannicus, son of Claudius and Messalina, can be no more than a hypothesis. We can be sure that a statue of Polyphemus occupied the centre of the apse, for there are two ledges to hold it in place, but the only trace of it seems to be a fragment of a lock of hair. The Cyclops was probably seated on a rock, as in the group in the pediment of the Temple of Dionysus standing in the agora of Ephesus (circa 40 BC). There the scene adorned a temple built by Marcus Antonius, the father of Antonia Minor. It was reproduced over and over again, in sculptures, bas reliefs, paintings and mosaics, up until the last decades of the Imperial period. We know that the statue of

Polyphemus had already been removed by the 5th century, when an amphora of African provenance was placed here containing the corpse of a baby. The nymphaeum must already have been abandoned, although this part of the exedra had not yet been submerged by the sea. The nymphaeum had a channel running round three sides beneath the recesses, with water flowing along it and catching the water spouting from the statues that doubled as fountains (Ulysses and his companion and both figures of Dionysus). A horseshoe-shaped platform stood above the large rectangular pool, which in the display is represented by the back-lit blue crystal flooring. At either end of the platform there were two large backrests from couches (*klinai*) made of marble and decorated with a horse in bas relief, the head seen full on. On the

between the apse and the recesses flanking it). Their decoration is particularly sophisticated: only a few elements have come down to us from the oldest phase, displayed in showcase 1. There was polychrome mosaic using vitreous paste with seashells set into it on the entrance wall and beneath the recesses. The recesses and apse were clad with lumps of limestone for added realism in this artificial grotto. The channel, pool and platform were faced with white marble, and this was probably also the case for the pilasters between the recesses. Above the recesses there seems to have been a horizontal frieze in *opus sectile* (inlaid polychrome marble) of which fragments have been retrieved including plant motifs and dancing couples facing each other. This particular decoration was further elaborated in the *Domus Transitoria* used by Nero in Rome, which indicates the existence of a specialised workshop catering for imperial commissions. The nymphaeum remained in use over a long period, even though some structural modifications and evidence of

ground there were a series of grooves to take the wooden backrests of additional couches, making it clear that this chamber was in fact a *stibadium* (nymphaeum-cum-dining room) where the emperor would have entertained his guests. It is in fact very similar to the nymphaeum-grotto built by Tiberius at Sperlonga in both its layout (on a somewhat smaller scale) and the Homeric theme. Its earlier counterpart featured the blinding of Polyphemus, and once again the statue of the Cyclops disappeared for good. The two groups of extant sculptures were produced in the same workshop, which took as prototypes Hellenistic sculptures from the school of Pergamon dating from the first half of the 2nd century BC. The technique is also Hellenistic, for the sculptures came in various sections, assembled by means of metal pins. The walls were built in either *opus reticulatum* (recesses, exedra and sides of the water channel) or *opus latericium* (front wall and the wall

Portrait-statue of Antonia Minor and detail of the face, from the Nymphaeum of Punta Epitaffio

Statue of Dionysus with the panther, and detail of his hair style, from the Nymphaeum of Punta Epitaffio

restoration work to the sculptures, such as lead being poured in round the metal pins, suggest that bradyseism had caused serious damage. Towards the end of the 3rd century AD the original mosaic decoration was carefully stripped off and replaced by slabs of white fluted marble surmounted by Corinthian-style calyx capitals. From then onwards the monument was gradually abandoned on account of the rising water, which to judge from the corrosion must have reached the recesses and the bases of the statues. All the serviceable material was removed (water pipes, marble slabs and cornices from the wall facing, much of which had been deposited in one place awaiting re-use). All that was left undisturbed was the cladding of the channel and the pool, presumably either too worn or too thin to be worth removing. The statues seem to have remained in position until the oxidisation of the pins caused the extremities (fingers and toes) to drop off. These were found in fragments in the channel beneath a deposit of miscellaneous rubble used to fill in both the channel and the pool.

When the statues themselves collapsed, either because they were knocked down or as a result of bradyseism, their fall was cushioned by the water which had already submerged much of the nymphaeum. Subsequently the whole area was levelled off with infill made up of building rubble and ceramic discards. It may have been during a period of quiescence of the bradyseism, and certainly after the removal of the statue of Polyphemus, that some burials took place in the apse. The gold coin on display was found in one of these in 1969. Minted in the reign of Justinian (527-565), it gives a definite indication of when the nymphaeum was definitively abandoned.

The showcases display a selection of the items found, arranged in chronological order. The earliest phase, the Julio-Claudian era, is represented by fragments of the polychrome mosaic that originally decorated the recesses, and of images in coloured marble from the frieze in *opus sectile* that ran round the walls above the recesses. The other finds date from the final period prior to the nymphaeum falling into oblivion, and include ceramic fragments from fine tableware and coarser kitchenware, oil lamps, amphoras, and two fragments of sculptures: the lower part of a male figure and part

Statue of a girl, from the Nymphaeum of Punta Epitaffio. Here the figure is shown integrated with the fragment of a hand and butterfly (symbol of psyche, the soul), *as if at the moment life departs*

Dionysus wearing a wreath of oak, and his face seen in close up, from the Nymphaeum of Punta Epitaffio

of a right arm bent at the elbow. Andreae attributed these respectively to statues of Augustus and Drusus (father of Claudius), which he believed to be two of the missing statues from the original layout.

From Baia to Bacoli

Bacoli (Bauli)

The place name *Bauli* derives from the legend of the stables (*boàulia*) that Hercules built for the oxen he had stolen from Gerione. For a long time the location of this Roman resort was a vexed question: it was often identified with Baia, but a careful reading of the references in Roman authors shows this to be wrong. Tacitus located *Bauli* between the headland of Miseno and Baia; Cassius Dio, in a passage describing the boat bridge built by Caligula between Puteoli and Bauli, gives its length as 3,600 Roman yards, 5322.60 metres, which corresponds to the distance between Pozzuoli and Bacoli. Like Baia, Bauli came under the jurisdiction of Cumae, and consisted mainly of the villas of wealthy incomers built between the 1st century BC and 4th century AD. Two famous properties belonged to the orator Quintus Hortensius Hortalus, with ponds for breeding moray eels, and Agrippina, killed on the orders of her son Nero by Anicetus, one of the officers of the imperial fleet. Both these properties were seized by Nero himself, and in fact Bauli, like Baia, was a resort for emperors and their entourages. Two inscriptions (CIL X, 1746 and 1747) speak of the *ordo* or *collegium Baulanorum*, a corporation of freedmen charged with administering the imperial estates. The stretch of coast between Punta del Castello and Marina del Poggio is covered with remains in *opus reticulatum* and *opus latericium* of *villae maritimae* built on the shore and now partly under water. In explorations of the seabed currently being supervised by Alessandra Benini in the southwest corner of the bay of Bacoli at Marina Grande, a large jetty in *opus caementicium* has been identified. Standing some 2 metres high, it was left without the usual cladding, and still contains one ring for a ship to berth. Above it there are the remains of a sumptuous villa: it is possible to identify the bath quarters, stretching back to the foot of the headland, although it is not clear how this part of the villa was linked to the part on land. In a little inlet at the back of the beach there is a large rectangular chamber, hollowed out of the tuff cliff with integrations in *opus reticulatum*. The apse in the far wall and recesses along the side

"Tomb of Agrippina",
view of the arena

walls identify it unmistakeably as a nymphaeum, built to the same design as that at Punta Epitaffio. The only Roman buildings which have been preserved and can be visited only this stretch of coastline are the so-called Tomb of Agrippina and the reservoir known as Cento Camerelle.

The "Tomb of Agrippina"

Local folklore has conserved the memory of Nero's act of matricide by referring to this building as Agrippina's tomb. The act itself was certainly terrible: the emperor first tried to have her drowned in a staged shipwreck, and when she saved herself by swimming ashore she was killed by his emissaries. In fact the building is what remains of a small theatre (*odeion*) belonging to a *villa maritimae*; precious little else of this villa is still to be found on the hillside behind. The original layout of the theatre dates from the early years of the 1st century AD: it was subsequently transformed into a large exedra serving as a

nymphaeum, probably as a result of the rise in the sea level. The original terraces were eliminated, and only a few traces of them can still be identified. There are three semicircular levels, blocked off to the north by a modern construction. The best preserved is the lowest level, now lying beneath the level of the beach. It gives access to a corridor, the rear part of which has been destroyed. The stucco work on the ceiling features a geometric design divided lengthwise into three: in the central section large medallions alternate with ribbed elements in square cornices. All the sectors were once adorned, but now it is only possible to make out reclining female figures holding out a dish with offerings, sea monsters, swans and dolphins. These are all motifs evoking water, as befits a venue for spectacles involving fountains and water features. This structure can be dated to the mid-1st century AD on the basis of stylistic affinities with the stucco work in

Cento Camerelle, the lower level of watertanks

the "Rooms of Venus" in the Archaeological Park of Baia; the decorative schemes may well have been produced in the same workshop. The middle level, also with a barrel vaulted roof, has windows and doors opening onto the stage area and serves as the substruction for the terraces, scant remains of which can be seen on the top, reached by two small steps. The upper level, of which only the inner wall survives,

decorated with brick semicolumns surmounted by parts of Corinthian capitals, was divided up into small chambers by partition walls when the theatre was turned into a nymphaeum and the terrace was replaced by water tanks.

The "Cento Camerelle"

The local name, "the hundred cubbyholes", conveys the impression of a labyrinth, but in fact this construction consists of a series of watertanks on two levels, each with its own alignment, hollowed out of a tuff cliff rising sheer out of the sea. A few metres below the second level there are signs of a third level comprising tunnels matching those immediately overhead. Only the top two levels are accessible, and the different alignment led Amedeo Mauri to maintain that there was once a villa standing on top of the second level. There are in fact some remains on the hillside behind of rooms in *opus reticulatum* and of fishponds, now partly under water. Some scholars have identified these remains with the villa that the orator Quintus Hortensius Hortalus is known to have owned "*ad Baulos*". The upper level, aligned north-east/south-west and dating from the 1st century AD, comprises four parallel corridors clad with *opus reticulatum* with tuff wedges covered in a thick layer of waterproof *cocciopesto* (crushed terracotta). The barrel vaults are supported by large arches, and in the centre of the roof there is a round skylight. The lower level, aligned roughly north/south, goes back further to the 2nd-1st century BC. The subterranean tunnels are disposed on a grid, the walls in *opus caementitium* faced in waterproof *cocciopesto* and with a projecting string-course typical of watertanks. There are narrow passageways between the tunnels, some surmounted by pitched rooftiles and some flat-topped. Not all the tunnels are accessible, and the walls have the names of visitors from past centuries scrawled up in charcoal.

Miseno (Misenum)

Like Baia, the toponym Misenum is based on a mythological character. Strabo refers to Misenus as a companion of Ulysses (*Geographica* V, 4, 6), but in all other sources he is identified as the bugler of Aeneas who was drowned off this part of the coast and buried on the headland, which does in fact resemble a tumulus. Up until the Augustan age Misenum was part of the territory of Cumae. It must have been a redoubtable port, for Dioniges of Halicarnassus (I, 53, 3) mentions that it played a decisive part in the victory of the Cumans over the Etruscans in the naval battle of 474 BC. It obviously continued to be of strategic importance: three centuries later it was attacked by Hannibal as part of his campaign to lay waste the *ager Campanus* during the Second Punic War (Livy, Historiae XXIV, 13, 6). In the 1st century BC it became a resort, with many villas belonging to prominent Romans, including the celebrated residences of Lucullus and the *gens Antonii.*

The harbour owed its reputation to its two contiguous basins, the outer one serving as the port proper and the inner one for repairs and refitting. In about 10 AD Augustus made it the official base for the Roman fleet stationed in the Tyrrhenian Sea. The fleet had previously used the *Portus Iulius,* which had become impracticable, perhaps on account of bradyseism. This marked a new chapter in the history of Misenum, which was granted administrative autonomy. The area between the *Mons Miseni* (Monte di Procida) and *Promontorium Miseni* (Capo Miseno) was detached from the territory of Cumae. Misenum seems to have become a *municipium,* enrolled in the tribe of *Claudia* and subsequently established as a colony during the 3rd century AD. The fleet was styled *classis Misenensis* and then during the 2nd century AD *classis praetoria Misenensis*, meaning that, like the praetorian guard, it came directly under the emperor's command. Each of the Roman fleets was supervised by a *praefectus classis.* This was the office held by Pliny the Elder when he set out from Misenum in 79 AD to bring aid to the population living beneath Vesuvius, only to succumb himself at Stabiae during the famous eruption which destroyed the coastal cities.

The decline of Misenum started with the fall of the Roman Empire. By the 6th century it was no more than a *castrum* (fortified township), probably built on top of the Roman city. The fleet was transferred by the Ostrogoth ruler Theodoric to the capital of his kingdom, Ravenna. In the 9th century (846?) Misenum was sacked by the Saracens. As we have seen, much of the evidence of Roman life in Baia was lost as a result of both bradyseism and blatant indifference during modern times. The fate of Misenum was considerably worse. This was after all Rome's most important military port during the first three centuries of the Empire, a *municipium* with its own magistrates and priesthoods; yet precious little has survived the wholesale property speculation of the post-war decades. We are left with traces of three public buildings (the Sacellum of the Augustals, theatre and baths) which stood in the forum, on the narrow strip of land between the headland and the outer basin; two large reservoirs ("Piscina Mirabile" and "Grotta della Dragonara"); and scant remains of two villas and the *colombarii* for sailors from the fleet along the road to Cuma (now Via Mercato del Sabato) in the locality of Cappella. We are able to establish the location of the military and civilian quarters of the town, existing cheek by jowl in the small space available. The territory of Misenum included the headland of Monte di Procida, known as *Mons Misenus* or *Cumanus*, which was often confused with Capo Miseno, generally referred to as *Promontorium Miseni*. The agreeable climate and fertile soil of this headland attracted a number of rustic and residential villas, and these are now beginning to come to light.

The military harbour

The harbour comprised two basins, the outer one measuring about 2 kilometres in length and 250 to 500 metres across, the inner one being what today is known as Maremorto. They were joined by a canal, now below ground level, with a wooden bridge across it. The military quarters must have stood round the inner basin and included barracks, accommodation, logistical structures and stores catering for 6,000 servicemen, although now there are very few scattered remains above ground. Remains of buildings on Punta Sarparella, partly underwater, led

Beloch to identify this as the residence of the commander of the fleet, occupying a strategic position overlooking the port. Other scholars locate it either on the islet of Pennata (Zevi Gallina 1970) or on Punta Terone (Vergara Caffarelli 1940). Another debated issue is whether the toponym Miniscola (or Miliscola) derived from *militum schola* (in the sense of parade ground). It applies to the sandbar linking Miseno with Monte di Procida, and the military association was reinforced by the discovery during the 18th century of an epigraph recording a *Schola Armatur(arum)*.

We are currently acquiring more information from systematic underwater investigations in the outer basin of the military harbour. Beloch drew attention to the remains of *pilae* (staggered concrete blocks acting as breakwaters) protecting the two moles at the entrance to the port, built out respectively from Punta Terone and Punta Pennata. The latter is no longer strictly a point, having become separated from the land during storms in November 1967. Off Punta Terone there is a double row of *pilae* varying in height between 3 and 6 metres, running northwards towards the port entrance. The arches joining the blocks supported the mole, the only part of which now visible is the mole-head (the rest having been incorporated into the modern breakwaters) with the remains of four stone mooring rings still attached. On the inner side of the mole there is a flight of steps used for embarkation. Close by the mole a large area comprising architectonic structures and heterogeneous material is being

excavated. The structures are not in fact where they originally stood, but accumulated here during dredging of the seabed, probably when the port of Miseno was used as a submarine base. This area has already yielded important finds, on display in the Archaeological Museum of the Phlegraean Fields: the bust of the "Hera Borghese" Aphrodite, displayed in the Room of the Plaster Casts; a male figure clad in a toga; two plinths originally bearing honorary statues with inscriptions, one the dedication by the local guild of fish merchants to *Caius Iulius Maro*, an official (*scriba*) employed in the administration of the fleet; and last but not least a copy (the third known to us) of the Aspasia of Kalamis. Off Punta Pennata there was a single row of *pilae* also projecting into the port entrance. There is a striking similarity between this layout and the famous fresco from Stabiae now in the National Archaeological Museum of Naples showing two moles and a port with two basins, although the scene has invariably been identified as Puteoli.

In the inner basin there must have been ships riding at anchor, but here the severe pollution makes it is impossible to carry out underwater explorations. Fortunately we can acquire a lot of information about the fleet and its crews from hundreds of inscriptions taken from the colombarii along the road from Misenum to Cumae, now Via Mercato del Sabato, and also from letters written on papyrus scrolls by sailors (*classiarii*) to their families. Originally the sailors were freed men and slaves from the Imperial household; as time went

on they were increasingly foreigners from the eastern provinces, Egypt and Thrace. Service in the navy was rewarded with payment, part in cash and part as a final lump sum. The duration was initially 26 years, subsequently extended to 28. On finishing, servicemen acquired Roman citizenship, which passed to their descendants, and the right to marry. It was common for sailors to choose to retire to a place where they had already formed a stable relationship. We know the names of some 90 ships, mostly named after divinities. Ships came in a whole range of sizes, from massive vessels with six banks of oars (*hexeres*) to small, fast-moving craft with two banks (*liburna*); Pliny was carried across the Bay of Naples on one of the latter during the eruption of Vesuvius on August 24th 79 AD. The only large-scale ruins we have connected with the fleet are two reservoirs, one known as "Piscina Mirabile", built on the top of the hill to the east of Maremorto, and the other as "Grotta della Dragonara", beneath the headland of Miseno on the shore of Miliscola. Ships could moor off the latter reservoir to take on water, presumably using an inlet which is now silted up. On the top of Punta del Poggio there are some remains which Mauri believed to be the ancient Lighthouse of Misenum.

The "Piscina Mirabile"

Eighteenth century scholars dubbed this structure the "wonderful pool" for its sheer size: it is one vast enclosure, measuring 70 m. in length, 25.50 m. across and 15 m. high. Hollowed out of the tuff cliff, it had two entrances reached by steps in the northwestern and southeastern corners, the latter now blocked up. Four rows of twelve pillars each support the barrel vaulted roof,

Mosaic floor from one of the rooms added on to the Piscina Mirabile

brought here by the aqueduct of the Serino, delivered to the northwestern corner. It can be confidently dated on the basis of the construction techniques: *opus reticulatum* with courses in brickwork for the walls, and small blocks of tuff for the pillars, all covered with a thick layer of *cocciopesto* for waterproofing. The central transverse corridor was set approximately one metre below the level of the others and sloped towards a hole in the southern side, serving as a decantation tank (*piscina limaria*) for the periodic draining of the reservoir. The water was drawn up by mechanical means through a series of hatches in the roof of the central corridor to the flat area above, also floored in *signinum*, and piped to the naval enclave. The capacity of the reservoir has been calculated at 12,600 cubic metres, which must have met the requisites of the naval base.

During the 1st century AD twelve small rooms were added along the northeastern wall, built in *opus mixtum* (*reticulatum* interspersed with brick courses) with vaulted

forming five corridors lengthwise and thirteen crosswise, giving the structure the imposing majesty of a cathedral. It was built in the Augustan age to store the water

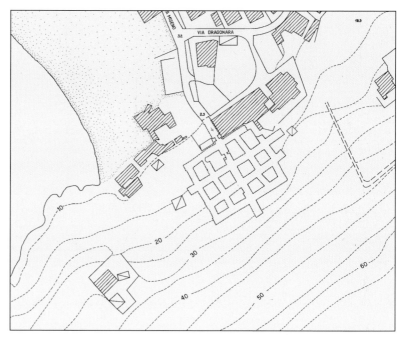

ceilings. In the second one along there is still the flooring in *signinum* with mosaic tesserae laid out in a labyrinth design and a centrepiece in white tessellae with polychrome limestone flakes, apparently dating from somewhat earlier.

The "Grotta della Dragonara"

This reservoir was even larger than the one described above (measuring approximately 70 x 44 m.), although it now lies about 3 metres below the original ground level and some of the tunnels have been destroyed. It was supplied by a fresh water spring still exploited in the Middle Ages and referred to by Pietro da Eboli in *De Balneis Puteolanis* as the *Fons Feniculi* (spring of the fennel) on account of the fields of fennel all around. It remained active until quite recently. The reservoir was hollowed out of the tuff on a grid pattern with twelve massive pillars forming five corridors and supporting the barrel vaulted roof.

In its current state its height varies between 3.50 and 7 metres. It too dates from the Augustan age, with walls in *opus reticulatum* covered in waterproof *cocciopesto*. The current entrance was created in modern time. Access was originally from the top through three large holes in the roof provided with flights of steps. Other skylights were bricked up in modern times. During recent excavations the three large holes were completely disengaged from the accumulated earth. It was found that the first two had tanks clad in waterproof *cocciopesto* accessible by a flight of steps. The bottom of the tanks sloped towards a hole emptying into the reservoir below. They must have been used to decant the rainwater collected by the reservoir and also to introduce fresh air. In the 4th-6th century AD the tanks fell into disuse and were used for humble burials, but the spring continued to be exploited in medieval times, as shown by a

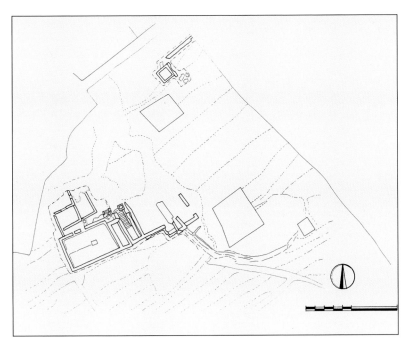

stone basin. The reservoir must originally have been designed to provide water for the fleet. When the capacity of the Piscina Mirabile was found to be sufficient, this structure was incorporated into the adjacent property known as the "Villa of Lucullus" (see below). Recent excavations have shown that the two sites were connected.

The "Villa of Lucullus"
Via Dragonara, Proprietà Salemme, near n° 6 (Ristorante Dragonara).
Due to open to the public, administered by Associazione Misenum
(081-5233977)

Recent excavations undertaken by Paolo Caputo on the hillside overlooking the Grotta della Dragonara have brought to light remains of a villa built on terraces overlooking the sea. Of the two groups of buildings so far identified, the older one can be dated to the 1st century AD and extends over the second and third large skylights in the roof of the reservoir. At present it is known to consist of a large semicircular wall in *opus reticulatum*, probably a nymphaeum that could draw on an abundant water supply from the reservoir below. There are likely to be other residential structures to the south and west, while on the higher terraces no buildings have been discovered. The other group, dating from the 2nd-3rd century AD, extends westwards from the nymphaeum, with structures clad in *opus vittatum* (courses of rectangular tuff blocks). Featuring numerous channels but no decorations, apart from one room with a floor in *signinum* (*cocciopesto* with mosaic tesserae inserted), these were probably service rooms.

Other remains scattered along the foreshore are difficult to decipher because they lie buried in up to 4 metres of sand. In the courtyard of the Ristorante Dragonara a rectangular chamber can be made out, hollowed out of the tuff cliff, with traces of plasterwork and a vaulted ceiling held up by a series of brickwork arches which divide up the interior into alcoves. It is shown in an engraving by Sadeler (circa 1606), and appears to have been either a nymphaeum or a steam bath. In the sea there are remains of fishponds and structures in *opus reticulatum* and *latericium*, with only the vaults showing above the seabed. This was obviously a large *villa maritimae*, traditionally identified with one known from literary texts to have stood on the crest of the headland. This belonged to Caius Marius and was purchased by Cornelia, the daughter of Sulla, at the knock-down price of 75,000 sesterces during the proscriptions imposed

Roman lighthouse at Miseno, ground-plan

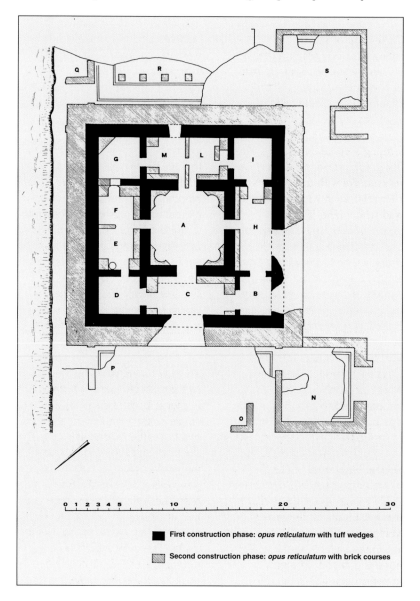

First construction phase: *opus reticulatum* with tuff wedges

Second construction phase: *opus reticulatum* with brick courses

by her father. It was subsequently acquired by the proverbially wealthy Lucius Licinius Lucullus for 2,500,000 sesterces (Pliny, Naturalis Historiae, XVIII, 32). On his death the villa became imperial property, and it was here that Tiberius died in 37 AD (Tacitus, *Annales* VI, 50).

The "Roman Lighthouse"
Via Pennata 74, proprietà A.M. Maddalena.
Due to open to the public.

On the top of Punta del Poggio, facing the open sea and the island of Capri, there are some remains of a square building with a central chamber (A) with three smaller chambers opening off it, all four culminating in segmental vaults forming a common roofing. This first construction phase in *opus reticulatum* with tuff wedges was later reinforced with a thick outer wall with a core of *opus caementicium* and cladding in *opus reticulatum* with brick courses. The central chamber was reinforced with stone curbs at the corners and other modifications were carried out in the smaller chambers, including the opening of skylights in the vaults. Four square outbuildings were added on at each corner. Today the whole structure is largely underground and inaccessible. It was believed by Mauri to have been the base for the lighthouse of Misenum, situated opposite the ancient lighthouse of Capri. This hypothesis was rejected by Anna Zevi Gallina, who argued that it was too distant from the port of Misenum, indicating Punta Pennata as a more suitable location. The hope is that archaeological investigations will be able to establish the true whereabouts of the lighthouse.

The *Municipium*
The town of Misenum occupied the narrow area between the western slopes of Capo Miseno and Punta Sarparella, overlooking the outer basin of the port. While we have an abundance of inscriptions concerning the fleet, we have very few about the workings of the *municipium*. It was run by the *curator rei publicae*, and other public offices were the *decuriones*, responsible for administrative matters, *duoviri quinquennales*, magistrates elected for a five-year term of office, and *sacerdotes*, responsible for the municipal cult. A further office of great distinction was that of priest in the college of the Augustals, administering the cult of the Emperor. The only public monuments to have come down to us are the Baths, the Sacellum of the Augustals and the Theatre.

The Public Thermal Baths
Via Dragonara 72, property of Nicola Cudemo. To visit contact Associazione Misenum (081-5233977)

These baths had two chambers, the *calidarium* and *praefurnium*. The former is large and square with an ample rectangular exedra at the far end beneath a segmental vault. The pool, which occupies the whole interior, is linked to the *praefurnium* in the cliff face at the rear. The walls of the chamber are built in brickwork and have been conserved up to the springer of the vaults. These were built with a double shell to allow hot air to circulate: fed between the

Miseno, Public baths, calidarium

Sacellum of the Augustals, axonometric reconstruction. The numbers indicate the plinths from the Sacellum displayed in a courtyard of the Archaeological Museum of the Phlegraean Fields in the castle of Baia

suspensurae holding up the floor, the air rose inside the walls through terracotta *tubuli*. The *praefurnium* was hollowed out of the tuff and roofed with overarching barrel vaults supported by brickwork arches. One can still see where the boiler stood, with a stone staircase leading down to it for maintenance work. The baths date from the first half of the 2nd century AD and remained in use until the 4th century AD, when the site probably began to sink as a result of bradyseism. Later on two kilns were installed in the north part of the *praefurnium*. The one dating from the 6th-7th century produced a type of amphora known as "misenate"; one complete specimen, together with many other finds, is on display in the museum. The other one, dating from the 11th-12th century, shows that craft work continued even at a time when the sea level was rising fast.

The Sacellum of the Augustals
Via Miseno, next to n° 233. To visit contact Associazione Misenum (081-5233977)

We have already illustrated the decoration and sculptures belonging to this monument in our description of the Archaeological Museum of the Phlegraean Fields above. The site lies at the foot of Punta Sarparella and was discovered in 1968 by Alfonso de Franciscis. It is one of the most interesting monuments known to us connected with the Imperial cult. The inscriptions found here tell us a lot about how the cult was organised and the personal fortunes of the Augustals, who constituted a hierarchical priestly

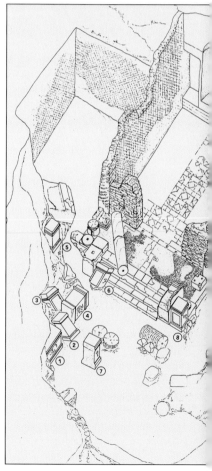

class, as well as many details concerning the history of Misenum. Much of it still remains to be investigated because it lies below sea level; we know that there was an area surrounded by porticoes, of which so far only the eastern side has been partially explored. At the far end there was a central chamber dedicated to the cult itself with service rooms on either side. The different construction techniques indicate at least three phases in the monument's history. The original nucleus, in *opus reticulatum*, dates from the early part of the Imperial era and comprises the central chamber and the western service room. At this time the chamber was preceded by a colonnade in *opus latericium* which was joined, at least on the eastern side, to a portico. During the 1st century AD refurbishing took place, and the walls of the eastern service room were lined in *opus vittatum* (rectangular tuff blocks), incorporating two of the columns in the portico. An inscription set into the mosaic flooring in front of this room records that this refurbishing was financed by the Augustal Quintus Baebius Natalis, and there is a similar inscription naming another benefactor in front of the western service room. In the second half of the 2nd century AD the façade of the temple was restructured. A large inscription set up in the lower cornice of the tympanum proclaims that this work was paid for by the priestess Cassia Victoria, in her own right and on behalf of her husband Lucius Lekanios Primitivus. Husband and wife are shown in the style of an Imperial couple in a relief on the pediment, and the text specifies that they wished to place on record the benevolence of the Augustals. The monument seems to have continued in use up to the Severian era (first half of the 3rd century AD), for this is when the statue of Fortune and the slab showing Oceanus and the chariot of Helios date from (both on display in the Museum). Subsequently, perhaps because of an earthquake, the building collapsed and was crushed by landslips affecting large sections of the cliff to the east. It is certain that the statues which were not buried were retrieved: one plinth which had been reused but is known to have come from this shrine was

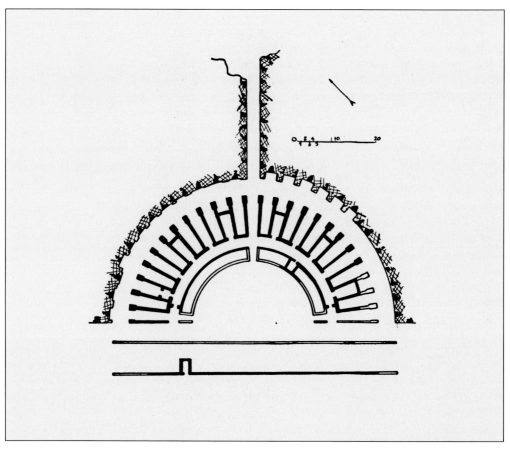

Theatre of Miseno, ground-plan of the whole building. All that can be seen today are the entrances to 19 radiating corridors and the straight gallery leading to the sea

found during the 18th century (plinth 11 in the Museum). The only statues which were completely engulfed were those standing in the shrine itself, and also some female figures and part of the equestrian statue of Domitian/Nerva, undoubtedly the masterpiece of the collection (see presentation of the Archaeological Museum of the Phlegraean Fields).

The Theatre
Via Miseno, n° 201. To visit contact Associazione Misenum (081-5233977)

The theatre stood next to the Sacellum of the Augustals. It is partly masked by modern buildings but what is visible can be readily

identified: some sections of the galleries in the substructions and the access to the terraces, which at the highest point were built against the hillside of Punta Sarparella. It is possible to enter the lower gallery, semicircular with barrel vaults, hollowed out of the tuff and clad in *opus vittatum* (rectangular tuff blocks). It now lies half-way below ground as a result of bradyseism. The entrances to 19 of the 25 radiating corridors are visible, although blocked with sand and walled up. They were faced with brickwork arches and led to another semicircular gallery further in. Beyond the central corridor there was a straight gallery, also now half blocked up, which presumably provided direct access to the sea. Since there is a gap of some 6 metres between the bottom of this gallery as it now lies and the sea level in Roman times, only underwater explorations will be able to establish the existence of the jetty and flights of steps one would expect to find at the end of the gallery. The area lying on private property (D'Albora) contains a short stretch of the upper gallery and, higher up, the remains of a brickwork arch and flight of steps. This probably led up to the *summa cavea*, the highest sector of terraces. The construction technique used indicates that the theatre was built in the 2nd-3rd century AD. The only plan we have of the whole monument was drawn up by Pali in 1768 and brought up to date by Vergara-Caffarelli in 1940. It gives the diameter of the orchestra as about 30 metres, and of the theatre as a whole as 71 metres. It seems unlikely that the equestrian statue of Domitian/Nerva, found in fragments below here in the Sacellum of the Augustals, originally stood in the theatre.

The colombarii

The Roman necropolises lie outside the towns, on the roads leading from Baia and Miseno to Cuma. The individual burials could take the form of simple tombs surmounted by a pitched tiled roof, urns bearing the cremated body, or funerary monuments. The most common type of the latter during the 1st and 2nd century AD was the colombarium, consisting normally of an underground chamber surmounted by a dome, with niches in the walls holding the urns of family members. These were usually accompanied by a funerary inscription giving the names of the deceased and the dedicant and details of the social status of the deceased. Many of those buried in these necropolises had served in the Imperial fleet stationed at Misenum. During the 19th century these tombs were dug up, above all for the sake of the inscriptions, and few additional remains have come to light. The two main groups of tombs lay outside the town of Misenum, one on the road to Cuma, on the western shore of Maremorto, in the locality Cappella, a toponym which records the ancient practice of burial here, and the other on the road to Bauli, now Via Roma. According to a survey carried out by A. Parma, no less than 569 funerary inscriptions are known to us from these necropolises, more than three quarters of them commemorating navy personnel. Regrettably practically nothing remains of the two sites, apart from scant traces along the road between Miliscola and Monte di Procida. The two best preserved funerary monuments are located elsewhere: in Via Scamardella, on the ancient route from Baia to Bauli, and in Via Fusaro, which runs from Baia via Lake Fusaro to Cuma.

The Columbarium of Via Scamardella
Via Scamardella 17. Private property.
To visit contact Ufficio Beni Culturali, Comune di Bacoli (081-8687641)

This funerary monument comprises three underground chambers. A flight of steps, incorporating the original one, descends to an

*The colombarium
in Via Scamardella*

*The colombarium
in Via Fusaro,
ground-plan
and cross-section*

arched passageway leading into the main, rectangular chamber. The walls are plastered up to a height of 1.60 metres, above which a section of wall in *opus reticulatum* is visible, continuing in *opus vittatum* (alternate tuff blocks and brickwork) for another 2 metres. Above this the walls are constituted by the tuff rockface itself up to ground level. The walls running lengthwise have four rows of niches. The main chamber led through into a small rectangular area, with another alcove above it. In the main chamber there are two square openings and a recess lined in brick where the sarcophagus would have been deposited. This monument can be dated to the 1st-2nd century AD.

The Columbarium of Via Fusaro
Via Fusaro 86. Municipal property. *To visit contact Associazione Legambiente (081-8688877)*

This underground burial chamber was discovered in 1841. Externally it is square with a flat top with ramps. Below ground there is a small round vaulted chamber in brickwork with a round skylight (*opaion*) at the centre of the dome. The interior wall has a striking design with projections and recesses, with four alcoves between the floor and ceiling, each provided with four rows of niches to take funerary urns. The interior is covered with white plasterwork, with white tesselated flooring. Access is down a short flight of steps, preceded by a small passageway with other niches, possibly intended for the mortal remains of freedmen of the family. This leads into a tiny rectangular vaulted alcove with niches in the walls and a rectangular recess to take a sarcophagus in the left wall. The columbarium stands in a large rectangular enclosure in *opus mixtum* (*reticulatum* with brick courses) with stuccoed semicolumns along the side walls. Inscriptions identify the monument with the *gens Grania*, and it can be dated to the central decades of the 2nd century.

Bibliography

**Miscellaneous works
(Baia and Miseno)**
J. Beloch, *Campanien. Geschichte
und Topographie des antiken
Neapel und seiner Umgebung*,
Breslau 1890.
M. Borriello - A. d'Ambrosio, *Baiae-
Misenum (Forma Italiae. Regio
I,XIV)*, Firenze 1979.
F. Ceci, s.v. Miseno, *EAA*, 1971-1994.
*I Campi Flegrei nell'archeologia e
nella storia*, Atti del Convegno dei
Lincei, Roma 1977.
I Campi Flegrei, Napoli 1987.
J.H. D'Arms, *Romans on the Bay
of Naples*, Cambridge (Mass.) 1970.
A. de Franciscis, *Baia, EAA*, Suppl.
1970, p. 133 ff.
A. Gallina, *Miseno, EAA*, Suppl.
1970, p. 495 ff.
R. Ling, *Stucco decorations at Baia*,
in *PBSR* 45, 1977, pp. 24-51.
A. Maiuri, *I Campi Flegrei*, Roma
1963 (V ed.).
M. Napoli, *Baia, EAA*, vol. I, p. 960 ff.
F. Zevi, *Baia, EAA*, Second Suppl.
1971-1994, p. 592 ff.
S. De Caro, *I Campi Flegrei, Ischia,
Vivara*, Napoli 2002.

Guides
P. Amalfitano, G. Camodeca,
M. Medri (edited by), *I Campi
Flegrei, un itinerario archeologico*,
Venezia 1990, pp. 185-263.
S. De Caro-A. Greco, *Campania,
Guide archeogiche Laterza*, Bari
1981, pp. 53-73.
F. Morghen, *Le antichità di Cuma
e Baia*, Napoli 1765.
P.A. Paoli, *Antiquitatum Puteolis,*

Cumis, Baiis, existentium reliquae,
Napoli 1768.

Geology, volcanology
L. Lirer, G. Rolandi, M. Di Vito,
G. Mastrolorenzo, *L'eruzione del
Monte Nuovo (1538) nei Campi
Flegrei*, in *Boll. Soc. Geol. It.*, 106
(1987), pp. 447-460.
A. Parascandola, *Il Monte Nuovo
e Il Lago Lucrino*, in *Boll.Soc. Natur.
in Napoli*, 55, 1946, pp. 151-312.
A. Scherillo, *Vulcanesimo e
bradisismo nei Campi Flegrei*,
in *I Campi Flegrei nell'archeologia
e nella storia*, pp. 81-116.
A.G. Segre, *La Carta batimetrica
n. 1256 I.I. del Golfo di Pozzuoli*,
Ist. Idrografico della Marina, 1972.

The Glass Flasks
S.E. Ostrow, *The Topography of
Puteoli and Baia on the eight Glass
Flasks*, in *Puteoli* 3, 1979, pp. 77-140.

From Lucrino to Baia
M. Pagano, *Il Lago Lucrino.
Ricerche storiche ed archeologiche*,
in *Puteoli-Studi di Storia Antica*,
7-8, 1983-84, pp. 113-226.
W. Johannowsky, *Appunti su
alcune infrastrutture dell'annona
romana tra Nerone ed Adriano*,
in *BA* 4, 1990, pp. 1-14.

Nymphaeum of Punta Epitaffio
B. Andreae, F. Zevi, *Gli scavi
sottomarini di Baia*, in *PdP*
XXXVII, 1982, pp. 114-156.
B. Andreae, F. Zevi (edited by),
Baia. Il ninfeo imperiale

sommerso di Punta Epitaffio,
Napoli 1983.
M. Gigante, *Thanatos e non Eros
a Baiae?*, in *PdP* XXXIX, 1984,
pp. 230-240.
F. Zevi, *Claudio e Nerone - Ulisse
a Baia e nella Domus Aurea*,
in *Ulisse. Il Mito e la Memoria*,
exhibition catalogue, Roma 1996,
pp. 316-331.

Baia underwater
G. Di Fraia, N. Lombardo,
E. Scognamiglio, *Contributi alla
topografia di Baia sommersa*, in
Puteoli-Studi di Storia Antica, 9-10,
1985-86, pp. 211-229.
G. Di Fraia, *Baia sommersa. Nuove
evidenze topografiche e monumentali*,
in *Archeologia subacquea. Studi,
ricerche e documenti*, I, Università
degli Studi della Tuscia - Viterbo,
Roma 1993, pp. 21-48.
N. Lamboglia, *Inizio dell'esplorazione
di Baia sommersa (1959-1960)*, in
*Atti III Congresso di Archeologia
sottomarina*, Barcelona 1961
(Bordighera 1971), pp. 225-249.
N. Lombardo, *Un documento
epigrafico dalla "Villa dei Pisoni" a
Baia*, in *Archeologia subacquea.
Studi, ricerche e documenti*, I,
Università degli Studi della Tuscia-
Viterbo, Roma 1993, pp. 49-63.
A. Maiuri, *L'esplorazione
archeologica sottomarina di Baia*,
in *Atti II Congresso di Archeologia
sottomarina*, (Albenga 1958),
Bordighera 1961, p. 108 ff.
F. Maniscalco, *Ninfei ed edifici
marittimi severiani del Palatium*

imperiale di Baia, addendum by A. Palma and F. Nasti, Massa Editore, 1997.
M. Napoli, *Di una villa marittima di Baia*, in *Bollettino di Storia dell'Arte del Magistero di Salerno*, 3, 1953, pp. 77-107.
E. Scognamiglio, *Il rilievo di Baia sommersa: note tecniche e osservazioni*, in *Archeologia subacquea. Studi, ricerche e documenti*, I, Università degli Studi della Tuscia - Viterbo, Roma 1993, pp. 65-70.

Thermal buildings
A. Maiuri, *Il restauro di una sala termale a Baia*, in *BA* 1930-31, pp. 241-253.
F. Rakob, *Litus beatae Veneris aureum. Untersuchungen am "Venustempel" in Baiae*, in *MDAI - RA* 68, 1961, pp. 114-169.
F. Rakob, *Römische Kuppelbauten in Baiae. Gewölbeprofile*, in *MDAI - RA* 95, 1988, pp. 257-301.
I Sgobbo, *I Templi di Baia*, in *I Campi Flegrei nell'archeologia e nella storia*, pp. 283-328.

Baia thermal baths
E.P. Auberson, *Etudes sur les thermes de Venus*, in *RAAN* 39, 1964, pp. 167-178.
R. Di Bonito, R. Giamminelli, *Le Terme dei Campi Flegrei*, Milano, Roma 1992.
L. Guerrini, *Copie romane del tipo Aspasia - Sosandra da Creta*, in *Antichità cretesi. Studi in onore di Doro Levi*, II, Catania 1974, pp. 227-234.
Le Terme Puteolane e Salerno nei codici miniati di Pietro da Eboli, Napoli 1995.
R. Ling, *The "Stanze di Venere" at Baia*, in *Archaeologia* 106, 1979, pp. 77-140.
A. Maiuri, *Terme di Baia. Scavi, restauri e lavori di sistemazione*, in *BA* 36, 1951, pp. 359-364.
M. Napoli, *Una nuova replica della Sosandra di Clamide*, in *BA* 39, 1954, pp. 1-10.
I. Sgobbo, *Terme flegree e origine delle terme romane*, in *Atti del I Conv. Naz. di Studi Romani*, Roma

1929, pp. 186-194.
I. Sgobbo, *I nuclei monumentali delle terme romane di Baia per la prima volta riconosciuti*, in *Atti III Conv. naz. studi romani*, Bologna 1934, pp. 294-309.

The Castle of Baia
A. Mauro, *Il Castello Aragonese di Baia*, Napoli 1979.

Baia plaster casts
C. Gasparri, *L'officina dei calchi di Baia*, in *MDAI RA*, 102, 1995, pp. 173-187.
Ch. v. Hees-Landwehr, *Capolavori greci in calchi romani*, Napoli 1984.
Ch. Landwehr, *Die antiken Gipsabgüsse aus Baiae. Griechischen Bronzestatuen in Abgüssen römischer Zeit*, Berlin 1985.

Bacoli - *Bauli*
History and topography
A. Maiuri, *Note di topografia campana: Bauli*, in *Rend. Acc. d'Italia*, Cl. Sc. Morali e Storiche, VII, vol. II, issue 9 (1941), pp. 1-12, now in *Itinerario flegreo*, Napoli 1984, pp. 159-168.
A. Benini, *Una villa marittima nelle acque di Bacoli. Note preliminari*, in *Atti del Convegno nazionale di Archeologia Subacquea*, Conference Anzio 1996, Bari 1997, pp. 193-202.

The 'Tomb of Agrippina'
A. Maiuri, *Il teatro-ninfeo detto "Sepolcro di Agrippina"*, in *Anthemon. Scritti in onore di C. Anti*, Firenze 1955, pp. 263-271, now in *Itinerario flegreo*, pp. 169-176.

Miseno
History and topography
A. Parma, *Classiari, veterani e società cittadina a Misenum*, *Ostraka*, III-n.1, giugno 1994, pp. 43-59. E. Vergara Caffarelli, *Note di topografia misenate*, in *Atti del V Congresso di Studi Romani*, Roma 1940 II, pp. 263-273.

The military harbour and the fleet
P. Caputo, *Attività di tutela della*

Soprintendenza Archeologica di Napoli e Caserta, in *Bollettino di Archeologia Subacquea*, Ministero per i Beni Culturali, II-III, nos. 1-2, 1995-96, pp. 237-241.
P.A. Gianfrotta, *Harbor Structures of the Augustan Age in Italy*, in *Caesarea Maritima. A retrospective after two millennia*, Leiden 1996, pp. 65-76.
M. Reddé, *Mare nostrum: les infrastructures, le dispositif et l'histoire de la marine militaire sous l'empire romaine*, Paris 1986.
V. A. Sirago, *Funzione politica della flotta misenate*, in *Puteoli* 7-8 (1983-84), pp. 83-112.

The 'Piscina Mirabile'
I. Sgobbo, *L'acquedotto romano della Campania*, *NS*, 1938, pp. 75-97.

The Sacellum of the Augustals
M. Bergmann, P. Zanker, *"Damnatio Memoriae" Umgearbeitete Nero-und Domitiansporträts. Zur Ikonographie der Flavischen Kaiser und des Nerva*, in *JDAI* 96, 1981, pp. 317-412.
G. Camodeca, *Iscrizioni nuove o riedite da Puteoli, Cumae, Misenum*, in AION ArchStAnt, n.s.3, 1996, pp. 149-173.
A. De Franciscis, *Il Sacello degli Augustali a Miseno*, in *Atti del X Convegno Magna Grecia*, Taranto 1970, pp. 431-452.
A. De Franciscis, *Il Sacello degli Augustali a Miseno*, Napoli 1991.
Domiziano -Nerva. La statua equestre. Una proposta di ricomposizione, Napoli 1987.

Public thermal baths
A. Cinque, F. Russo e M. Pagano, *La successione dei terreni di età post-romana delle Terme di Miseno (NA): nuovi dati per la storia e la stratigrafia del bradisismo puteolano*. in *Soc.Geol.Ital.*, Roma 1991, pp. 231-244.

The Columbarium of Via Fusaro
A. De Franciscis - R. Pane, *Mausolei Romani in Campania*, Napoli 1957.

Printed in October 2006
on behalf of Electa Napoli

Photocomposition: Grafica Elettronica, Naples
Photolithograph and printing: SAMA., Quarto (Naples)
Binding: Legatoria S. Tonti, Mugnano, (Naples)